MARINE PATROL

KAM R. JOHNSON

CONTENTS

TRUE STORIES AND INSIGHTS

From a Retired Florida Marine Patrol/ FWC State
Officer ~

Kam R. Johnson

MARINE PATROL

Copyright © 2022 Kam R Johnson.

ISBN:
979-8-218-04284-4
Library of Congress Control Number:
2022913846

"Reflections in the waves spark my memory"

(Lyrics, from the song COME SAIL AWAY by Styx.)

1

THE MANATEE CAPER

It was a hot and humid August afternoon in the Gulf of Mexico, about two miles offshore of Yankeetown, Florida. I was currently doing an unpleasant job. The stench was terrible, and as I powered the 21 foot marked patrol boat throttle with a 225hp Johnson motor faster with one hand, I pinched my nose with the other. I steered with my legs against the steering wheel until the breeze hid the stink of rotting flesh. In tow behind me was a large adult manatee that had been dead a long time. (Sometimes called Sea Slugs) It's amazing of the rumors drunk sailors long ago reported them as mermaids. The Manatee had been dead so long that the body had burst open with guts and stink in the hot sun. Its gray skin had begun to peel off, leaving bright white meat that was underneath. It was also bloated like a balloon. It was about six feet in length. An adult averages about 1200 pounds. Many times you can see them swimming with boat prop scars across their back. Of the hundreds of different job requirements of my position as a Marine Patrol Officer, one is to aid in bringing dead or injured marine life to shore. If alive (like manatees, sea turtles, injured birds, etc.) we try to get them help. If dead (like manatees or dolphins, etc.) we bring them to shore, so they can be picked up by a lab group from St. Petersburg, FL for a necropsy. They study the carcass to determine the cause of death as it is an endangered species.

As the patrol boat gained speed the smell became more tolerable. I had made my harness for these situations. I had clipped two lengths of rope about 10' in length from either side of my boat motor. Then I connected a single and much longer piece from the joined two pieces of rope on one end and tied the other to the fluke of the dead manatee floating in the water. I tried very hard to hold my breath with that part! When towing, the dead manatee gets pulled backward. I had used the harness many times before for things like this or disabled boaters. Back then we frequently would tow broken-down vessels back to shore as a courtesy. Later on however, due to liability, we had to refer them to Sea Tow or something similar. A lot of us continued to tow people in with short tows anyway, and not tell dispatch or supervisors. Especially if they were drifting, in bad weather, or posed a threat in busy channels. Always have an anchor and plenty of rope!

It goes without saying that I had to be careful not to entangle the rope in my boat prop before taking off. My training officer early on had cued me to always have a sharp knife, of course, and also wire cutters. Numerous times I have had to throw my anchor out in a river or channel on a busy weekend, tilt my motor up high, and lean out with one hand to cut rope or an abandoned wire blue crab trap that had wrapped around my boat prop. With the other hand, I had to hold on to something to keep from falling into the water from a rocking boat. It's hard to look cool and professional doing that with a uniform and gun belt on, all the while you are getting waked by people who are oblivious or gleefully getting revenge for a past ticket. When doing that, you have to also turn the prop by hand periodically to effectively cut the tightly wrapped wire or rope off that is all around the prop.

As the patrol boat gained more and more speed the dead manatee began to flop around and ski so to speak behind me. Truth be told I should be towing it at slow speed, but none of us did that. It would take hours and hours and the smell and attacking no-see-ums would be miserable. (" No-see-ums", also called "sand gnats") would fly around and sting your bare skin by the hundreds. It was the same with towing families from offshore in disabled vessels. We would have them sit down and put their life jackets on, hook up the harness, put our blue lights on, and slowly increase our speed, so much so that some of them had never reached that speed with their boat ever before! (Times were different then.) Most of the time they would be smiling and happy. They were headed home for free and getting a cool breeze now. I would swivel my head a hundred

times from front to back as I went along for safety, and
would notice them waving at me and happily chatting
among themselves about a story they now had to tell.
Most likely some were thinking of air conditioning and a
bathroom. Naturally, I slowed in the channel and then
tied to them side by side, both my patrol boat and theirs
next to each other. I then expertly would glide them up
to the dock by the boat ramp. They often shook my hand
and offered me money, which of course I declined. I
would not anyways, but it is against policy for us to take
gratuities. Some officers would do a full safety equipment check at that time, in hopes of getting activity,
(warnings and citations) which supervisors always
expects at the end of the month to show you are doing
your job. I never did in that situation, unless they did not
have life jackets to put on during the tow. It was nice for
a change for the public to smile at you in thanks, instead
of a frown from a ticket.

Anyways, back to finish this manatee caper! As the
boat hummed along at about 25 mph and making steering
adjustments from the weight of the flopping manatee, I
grabbed the radio mic with one hand and steered with the
other. With most boats there is no need to hold the
throttle down, it stays in place where you leave it. All good
boaters of course keep their hand on it, in case they need
to slow or even reverse hard quickly. There are no brakes
on a boat! "230 Crystal River," I said speaking into the
depressed radio mic.

"Go ahead 230" the voice on the mic replied.

"I'm 10-51 to Yankee Town boat ramp, manatee in tow.

10-52 about 30 mikes. What's the status of the biologist?" I asked.

"10-4, 230, go ahead and secure it there, they won't be able to retrieve it until morning" the dispatcher communicated.

I replied, "10-26" which means message received. I was actually glad to hear that because sometimes you had to babysit the dead manatee for an hour or more, and then have to help get the manatee into the back of the biologist's covered trailer at the ramp. They would attach a cable to the manatee fluke and hand crank it in like a boat trailer crank. I truly don't know how they stand the eye-watering smell, and I lived on a dairy farm!

I continued in the offshore crooked Withlacoochee boat channel with the boat ramp in sight. At night was very tricky, but even now in the late afternoon there could be cross currents and wakes from other sometimes larger vessels. As I slowed down getting within a hundred yards or further of the boat ramp, the horrible smell again kicked in. The tidal current was ripping outbound, and as I got closer about a million no-see-ums began to work on my arms and legs, as I was in shorts. There wasn't any wind to keep them off. I stupidly had forgotten my mixture of "Skin So Soft" oil and water, a 50/50 mixture in a spray bottle left in my patrol car. (Later we had patrol trucks). The mixture is sprayed on bare skin to block the no-see-ums stings, that leave red spots on your skin. Skin So Soft is actually a female Avon skin product, and according to my now deceased awesome father-in-law, made you smell like a " whore". I would have given ten bucks for two sprays at that time! The rotting carcass of the manatee was attracting every no see um in a mile radius it seemed! The insects are very tiny and don't really bite, it just stings when they touch your bare skin. The common joke is that if you look at one under a microscope it would have giant teeth! When there is no wind they get into your hair, ears, nose, etc... I probably have accidentally eaten thousands of them in my career. I'm not joking!

In complete torture of the dead manatee stench, and a cloud of no-see-ums stinging my unprotected skin, I squinted through my sweat and sunglasses towards the boat ramp situation. A sudden crazy idea came to my mind. Mentally I said, "screw this crap!" I suddenly gunned the boat forward causing the 225hp motor to roar, and as the patrol boat increased speed I was immediately rewarded with a stench-relieving cool salty breeze and disappearing no-see-ums out of my nose. The now clear boat ramp was fast approaching off my bow. I then suddenly slowed and sharply turned to starboard (right) and put the boat in neutral. I then grabbed my sharp folding knife out of my belt, and carefully turned and stepped to the stern (back) of the boat. The patrol boat was slowly coasting to the right still running, but out of gear. The momentum of my previous speed and stop had caused the dead manatee behind me to rapidly shoot towards the boat ramp. As I got slack in my boat harness I reached out and pulled some rope out of the water. I had to kneel on the deck and reach over the side. As the dead manatee rapidly went by I cut the harness as far out as I could. I then threw the remains of the harness into the boat so as not to entangle it with my prop, and punched the throttle forward heading outbound. The no-see-ums were horrible. As I left the area, I looked back and smiled. The fast-moving dead carcass glided perfectly up the wet and slippery boat ramp. Luckily, the tide even though receding was still high. The dead manatee became high and dry on the top of the boat ramp with some rope still attached to its fluke. A present for the next fisherman launching his boat, as has been many times before. Unfortunately, this one would be there until morning. The dispatchers no doubt would be getting many calls about it until picked up. It was a wide boat ramp so boaters could still use one side. Twelve hundred pounds of stinking rotting carcass and clouds of no-see-ums would keep others away. The buzzards would no doubt be on it before morning. I marveled at the dedication of those who do the necropsy!

I grabbed the mic and advised the dispatcher, "Crystal River 230, I'm 10-98, 10-51 back to Crystal River."

"10-4, 230," she replied.

I increased my speed and headed back to Citrus County homeward bound. It was past my shift and I still had to go through many zigs and zags offshore, whether it be channels, rivers, slow zones, sand bars, crab traps, or many other boaters. I had to retrieve my boat, unload my gear, rinse it off, and tow it home. Along the way, I didn't want to check any more boaters unless I saw something unsafe. I better not see any illegal speeding vessels in manatee zones as I head home though! Gee, I wonder why!

I should note that the gentle giants are truly amazing to watch. I have had many approach me in the water while snorkeling and enjoy me scratching its huge body. The rumors of the Florida Manatee not being original to Florida are not true. Many Florida biologists have told me that Manatee bones have been found all over in old Indian junk piles of oyster shells dated thousands of years ago.

2

___

LOCATION ASSIGNMENT

"Johnson, Steinhatchee! I recommend you go to the nearest tree and hang yourself. Or go down to the Highway Patrol Academy and sign up with them," chuckled one of my training Sergeants who just read out loud to me in class where my first assignment was. He was reading down the list while us new recruits were squirming in our seats praying. There were about forty-nine of us left that were going to graduate. We had put in our dream sheets earlier in the six-month Florida Marine Patrol Academy in 1989. Dream sheets were your top three choices of where you wanted to be assigned if you graduated. Some guys got their pick, some like me did not. I wanted Panama City, where the sand was white, the water was blue, and had lots of tan beautiful women. What can I say? I was single at the time!

The Sergeant continued calling out the assignments,

"Jones, Marathon. Harper, Miami. Morrison, Miami. Robert Miami." A lot of people going to Miami I thought. Steinhatchee? Where the heck is that? I was starting to sweat bullets. The Sergeant knew where or what it was, and I bet it wasn't on anybody's dream sheet!

I glanced at the guy next to me and he must have been reading the look on my face. "I passed Steinhatchee on Highway 19 coming up here," he said. "It's about a half-hour south of Perry, and if you blink an eye you'll miss it! The only thing there was a flashing yellow light!" he continued.

Man, it just gets better and better I thought. My whole body language must have had that depressing look because another guy behind me tapped me on the back and eagerly offered "Hey bro, I'll trade with you! I've got Miami." For a short time, we actually could trade up.

"I appreciate it, but I don't want Miami either!" I admitted. There was a lot of hubbub in the room after the Sergeant had finished reading the list. Now that the bomb was dropped, he left the room probably knowing there would be a combination of "yee haws" to mild cursing and "I quit" in the group. I don't know how assignments were chosen, only the dream sheets probably were used to get you close. A roll of the dice may be for the leftovers. I decided against Miami. I didn't speak Spanish and that was too far from Panama City. Besides, how bad could Steinhatchee be? It was a lot closer to Panama City than Miami. If I can get through lie detector tests, psycholog-ical tests (fruitcake tests/a three-hour test which can apparently tell if you would make a good officer), an oral review board, background checks, a six-month academy of five am yelling, running, push-ups, sit-ups, tower stair climbing, and all-around puking, then I can surely handle Steinhatchee. Anyone in FMP class 13 will tell you, no lie, we ran about thirteen miles the first day! We were one of the largest classes and I think the instructors wanted to show us who was boss right away. Additionally, we had classes from law to fish identification. Domestics to boating accidents, oil spills to navigation, recreational and commercial regulations. Too many classes to list. We also squeezed in hours of extreme driving, defensive tactics, handcuffing, and day/ night shooting. Some people little by little sadly were cut out due to injuries or failing tests. So I wasn't afraid of 'Steinhatchee', until my first trip to it anyways.

I only had one more week at the Academy (yeah!). Having the weekend clear most everyone bugged out early to scope out their assignment where they would have to stay for one year on probation. A new recruit also has to be trained, evaluated, and tested in the field by training officers (FTO) for about three months. Upon completion of that, you are on probation for a year. My FTOs, later on, told me to throw out almost everything I learned in the academy and to let the training officers tell me the real deal. Such as dealing with all kinds of people, courts, boat handling, paperwork, laws, and supervisors.

Anyway, I was headed to "Steinhatchee" in my personal car and in civilian clothes of course to scope it out and hopefully find some cheap place to rent, and boy do I mean cheap! I definitely wasn't going to get rich with this job! I drove south on Highway 19 through Perry, which took about a good hour and a half from the academy in Quincy. Perry is a small country town with a lot of true southern style. It unfortunately also had a strong sour paper mill smell which initially makes you want to continue to drive through. I bailed a lot of hay and shoveled a lot of cow manure on a dairy farm while growing up in Vermont, but that sour smell was nasty. So I kept trucking southbound to Steinhatchee. From there on out, there was nothing for miles and miles. Along the way, it became very foggy and I had to slow down. It was about nine in the morning and it was a cool December morning. It was weird because of the fog and being in Florida and not seeing anything for mile after mile except for pine trees, scrub brush, and the long straight foggy road. After about twenty minutes from Perry, I finally passed a large sign on the right of the road. It said, "Prepare to meet thy Maker". (An obvious church message) Now I'm beginning to feel like I'm in the Twilight Zone. After ten minutes of driving and seeing nothing I finally see a flashing yellow light with a small intersection. There was a bar on the left which most people I talked with later said it was the local knife and gun club. I turned right and took the curved fifteen-minute road into downtown Steinhatchee.

Finally, I made it to Steinhatchee! At that time in 1989, it was a very small fishing town, consisting of a small seafood restaurant, convenience store/gas station, elementary school, some river houses, trailers, and a marina.

There was no police station or medical office. Not much else in town. I went into the marina and bought a navigation chart of the area. Guess what the bay there is called on the chart at the mouth of the Steinhatchee River? "Dead Man Bay".... No, I swear everything I'm writing in this book is true. I was beginning to think I should have taken Miami. So let me recap. It was very foggy, I had seen a sign that said "**Prepare to meet thy Maker**", and the bay I'll be patrolling for at least a year in the middle of nowhere is called "**Dead Man Bay**". The words, "I'm not in Kansas anymore" went through my head. I had been in the Army as a Military Policeman for three years before the Florida Marine Patrol Academy, I'm six feet and was academy hardened, but I won't lie to you, I was feeling nervous. I had to live in Steinhatchee for a year. No other FMP Officer would be there, only two training officers that were in Keaton Beach, about twenty-five minutes north of me by the middle of nowhere shortcut. So I could forget back up.

I talked a bit with the marina manager. He told me the nearest grocery store was about forty minutes away in Cross City at the "Piggly Wiggly". He also advised me to buy some "Skin So Soft" made by Avon for the no-see-ums. You don't survive Steinhatchee and other Florida marsh areas unless you have a gallon of Skin So Soft which they get stuck to. I noticed in the marina also, that a lot of older posted fishing pictures from the area of times past. There was one picture of a giant "Jewfish", now called "Goliath Grouper" that was being hoisted by a crane at the marina from a large fishing boat. It was the size of a VW bug automobile, no exaggeration. As I looked around an older man walked in and began talking with the manager. The man had a throat device that was mechanical and worked on vibrations made from the throat when talking. He may have had throat cancer surgery and may God bless him, but the mechanical sound to me just added to the spookiness of the whole atmosphere.

I then went to the convenience store where they sold chicken gizzards by the bag full, which I thought was unique. I asked about any rentals or local newspapers and they said good luck finding a rental. Everything in that small town in 1989 was done by word of mouth. I also began my education on how the town had a lot of people on parole and recent jail releases from a huge Federal marijuana bust about ten years prior. Evidently, from the commissioner to the local Sheriff and many others in Steinhatchee were busted on a sting operation. Back then apparently, it was common to see lookouts and hear machine-gun fire at night. I heard a lot about that later from the locals and Taylor County deputies. You can go there today and still see the locally named "Road to nowhere" on the "Jena" side, which is miles long and lines up perfectly with the Horseshoe Beach Tower light at night. All compliments of that crooked commissioner and others who used it to offload large amounts of marijuana. At the academy, an officer remarked, "You'll own that town!" However, I was beginning to think the town would own me!

I tried again with the store clerk. "I can see it's going to be hard finding a place to rent quick. I'll be the new

Marine Patrol Officer assigned here and I'm graduating next week."

"Really? No kidding?" she said. "My husband and I boat a lot. So remember this face and don't write us any tickets!" she laughed. "My name is Sharla and if I hear something about a rental, I'll let you know."

"Okay, thanks! I'm sure I'll be seeing you." I said. As I started to leave, an older man in white boots with a weather-beaten face approached me who had come in as I was talking to the store clerk.

"Did you say yer the new Marine Patrol Officer going to be here?" He asked.

"Yes sir, I just came down here to find a place to rent first," I answered.

"Well I'll be durn, I heard you wus going to be a black woman!" the older man commented.

"Pardon me?" I asked.

He spits in a cup before replying "Yea, the word was the new Marine Patrol Officer here wus goin to be a black woman!" He then extended a calloused hand out to me. "My name is Hank, I've been a commercial fisherman here all my life. Where yer from?" Hank asked.

I shook his callused hand back. I introduced myself and explained I grew up in Vermont on a farm and came to Florida after getting out of the Army.

"Oh, so yer a Yankee!" He said as he smiled and spit in his cup again.

I had never been called a Yankee before, even in my last Army year in Alabama, and I was still wondering about his first remark about being a black woman. "A Yankee? I asked.

He chuckled, "nothing personal son, we call everyone north of Perry a Yankee."

"Ha, oh I see. Well, it probably doesn't help that I'm law enforcement either" I responded.

"Well, just don't write me any tickets and we'll get along fine," he said as he winked.

I saw some more guys in white boots in the parking lot and decided to leave before I got surrounded with questions. "Well, glad to meet you, sir, I need to get going back to Tallahassee." (Officers then jokingly called the Land of Oz) I'll see you later."

As I left, back towards Perry thinking about lunch, I pondered what the heck Hank had meant about me being a black woman? I figured finally that someone obviously was joking with him, by portraying the most opposite physical-like officer who in "his mind" would be most likely to be the least fair in enforcing laws.

I remembered my stepdad and other farm owners that I worked for who routinely had to have state inspections. It must be tough to work like a dog in all kinds of elements and then also have your bread and butter depend on the inspector who may or may not be fair. I told myself then I would kick butt when needed but would be fair and consistent as much as possible. I was worried about finding a place to rent, and even more worried about having to tell my younger brother who was going to room with me about Steinhatchee. We were expecting a place with white sand, blue water, and tan beautiful women. He came off the farm and roomed with me on the west coast of Florida when I got out of the Army. We both were trying to get careers going and split the rent while doing it. We ate macaroni and cheese and used cardboard boxes for furniture. Wait until he hears about the downtown armpit of the world Steinhatchee!

3

RUNNING RADAR

I was the rare one in my district who was trained and chose to consistently operate stationary radar in the various manatee speed zones of Citrus County. I had to attend a week-long intense radar school where I learned to operate it, test it, keep logs, do court testimony, get it certified every six months, and practice day and night at the school to estimate vehicle speeds. I had also operated radar in my last year in the Army. I won't get into laser and moving radar which the Highway Patrol uses. In a nutshell, you first visually estimate the speed of a moving target and see it is speeding. (Due to hours and hours of practice at the school, which the instructor verifies with a calibrated radar unit, I passed a day and night test with only the required variance of plus or minus two miles an hour! You had to be that accurate without a radar unit!) Only then are you allowed to point the radar unit at the target. In essence, you are supposed to use the radar unit to only verify and confirm your trained self-estimate. As you are tracking the target coming towards you the radar unit will produce a Doppler tone. A fast-moving target will make it scream. You then verify you are tracking the right target by noticing the Doppler tone change as it passes you by. If the tone stays consistent when the target goes by, then you are obviously not tracking that target. I was never worried, as I only did obvious ones and ones that I was 1000% positive. When I chased them down with blue lights and sirens, they never disputed me because they knew; hence, I very rarely had to go to court.

A quick note on the "Cosine Effect" as they call it. I always tried to put myself at the minimum angle to have the most direct line with targets. The greater the angle, the more the radar unit will indicate a slower speed than the target is actually going. This is always a benefit to the target. It makes it a challenge to do this, and not give away your presence. Some stops are exciting and end up in a chase, as many pretend they don't see or hear me as I'm doing fifty miles an hour beside them and trying to get their attention to pull over. This happens a lot with kids on jet skis or people with illegal fish, and they hope I can't go fast as they can, as they pretend to not see me and punch it. Some stops are also funny....

I was tied to a large dock on my starboard side, midway of Crystal River. I was bow out to take the many powerful boat wakes coming from many vessels going back and forth. Holiday weekends are crazy, especially during scallop season. As I glanced towards incoming vessels on my starboard side, I noticed right away a fast-moving bass boat throwing a rooster tail and passing slower vessels. I visually estimated its speed to be 45mph in the well-marked 25mph manatee zone, but then noticed it accelerating even more. I raised my calibrated radar gun and pointed it directly at it. It indicated 51mph as the Doppler tone screamed, and then changed as it passed by me. I quickly laid the handheld radar unit on my console by the windshield for safekeeping, it was going to get bumpy! I quickly uncleated my one rope tied midway for a quick getaway. I then turned on my blue lights and punched my throttle forward, causing my 225hp motor to roar and easily push my light 19 'pathfinder patrol vessel quickly into the bumpy chaos of large and small boats, jet skis, etc.. going back and forth in the narrow river. I had carefully observed my speeding targets' markings, color, description, as well as the operator and passengers. The registration number was too obscured in the low fast-moving boat with water splashing to see clearly. However, even if I lost my target briefly in the chaos I could easily identify the operator again. I turned on my siren also since there was so much boat traffic and I wanted to pass others safely. The siren is very loud, and rightfully so since boat engines can be loud. I always put my headphones on when operating, which protects my hearing, keeps my hat on, and I can hear the dispatcher through it. As with any chase of sorts, it is dangerous and all liability, was mine. A good thing about an officer's blue lights seen by the public is to indicate we are there doing our job and hopefully encourage the public to be lawful.

I gained speed and carefully passed the other boaters heading inbound. I continued to catch up as I could see the rooster tail from my target getting closer and closer. It was a fast bumpy ride, while sometimes hitting over fifty mph and shocking people with my blue lights and a loud siren. I had to go back and forth with my speed, and zig and zag carefully so as not to interfere with others with my wake. My target was not doing that, which made me contemplate careless operation to add to his violation. Of course, there is also always the possibility he may be drunk or have warrants, which is more common than you would believe. Many warrants are for "Failure to appear" or "Failure to pay child support". We then have to confirm by dispatch who double-checks with the agency that put out the warrant and then we haul them to jail. Sometimes the local S.O. (Sheriffs deputies) if not busy will kindly come and get them, as we have to secure their boat if a competent passenger isn't available.

I finally stopped my target in Kings Bay, and after shutting my siren off but leaving the blue lights on, I yelled "Shut your engine off captain!" He quickly complied, and as he and his shocked passengers looked nervous I quickly threw my black bumpers out and cleated his vessel to mine. We were now in an Idle zone and much calmer water. I had intentionally paused stopping him until he approached the Idle zone. This made the stop much safer and easier. It is very challenging and sometimes impossible to stop a boater in heavy traffic with bad wakes. As I surveyed them over for fishing knives, saltwater products, threats, their attitudes, empty alcoholic containers, etc... I also had to have my head on a swivel as we were still drifting and had to call it in.

"Two-thirty Crystal River 10-50. I said on the mic.

"Go ahead 230"

" It'll be registration Foxtrot Lima ...... adjacent to Buzzard Island in Kings Bay." (Dispatcher then will quickly give the vessel information, and if listed as stolen) I then gave my full attention to the operator.

"Good afternoon captain. I'm Officer Johnson of the Florida Fish and Wildlife Commission. Do you have any justifiable reason to operate 51mph in a well-marked 25mph manatee zone?"

His face and eyes were red from wind and sun, but I smelled no alcohol and his speech was clear but flustered.

"I didn't know about the speed, we are just heading to the boat ramp.

"Yes sir, the speed limit is 25mph, and you passed many large signs indicating such. Also, your wake was slamming into other boaters as you closely passed them at high speed. You are always responsible for your wake at all times, regardless of the location. I have seen people get hurt, or equipment damaged from bad boat wakes...May I see your driver's license and registration please?"

As he looked for it he replied almost angrily now..."How could I see the signs? I was going too fast!"

A passenger quickly piped up testily also. "Why the speed limit? Manatees can't read!"

I calmly retrieved the license and registration. The operator quickly fired another question. "Is a driver's license even required to operate a boat?"

They all glared angrier at me now for making a spectacle of themselves in front of a crowd with my blue lights on and expecting a ticket. I paused to fish out my ticket book. I then replied, "No sir, it's not required to have a driver's license, it just speeds things up so I don't have to verify everything with dispatch. I can't release you until I have a positive identity. Also, no offense sir, but if you told a Highway Patrol Officer you were going too fast to read the sign, would that be justifiable? He just glared at me as he could see me writing the ticket. "Lastly, before I bug you all to see your required safety equipment, the 25mph zones is to give the boater and manatee a chance to avoid each other better. The manatee has to come up for air about every 20 minutes, and its lungs are on top. So a blunt collision for the boat could kill it. To be honest, I also run radar to protect the manatee and people. I have a lot fewer accidents on holiday weekends doing so. Some jet skis can easily do over 70mph."

(I have done the above hundreds of times besides my other hundreds of responsibilities over two decades. It has entailed too many combinations to mention, but you get the idea now about running radar, many of which have occurred late at night, which is a whole new ball game, full of danger, lighting challenges, drunks, and bugs in the face.)

4

FOR THE BIRDS

I was on the day shift in Kings Bay one morning in the early winter. Many anchored boats with fishermen were there in the manatee idle zone since the cold weather had driven a lot of spotted seatrouts there from the Gulf to be in the warmer water generated from the springs. "Have a safe day" I said to the vessel I just checked and was slowly pulling away from. In verbal judo training we had, it was advised to say, "Have a safe day", rather than "Have a great day", when concluding a stop. The premise being if I had to write them a warning or a ticket, and said "Have a great day", it might sound condescending or sarcastic. Also, they may come back and say, "It was a great day until you came along!" When you say, "Have a safe day", it can't be made into a verbal weapon by the public.

I started to put up my black bumpers and head outbound, thinking everyone has seen me now and they would have gotten rid of any illegal fish or stopped fishing if they had no license as they all had seen me by now. (This is why I used my binoculars offshore to watch people fish and confirm their appearance from a distance, before charging at them with the sun behind my back. I then can require a fishing license even if they quickly drop the fishing pole when they see me coming. I'm not kidding!) We can also check all compartments mostly, and check for stringers hidden off the side of a boat, for fish, but surprise is always the best tool for law enforcement. We have to be proactive, there is no other way to protect the resources!

Anyways, as I started to leave the area a nearby fisherman in a boat was waving hard at me to come over. I left my bumpers out and Idled towards him. As I approached I noted his anchor line and expertly avoided it, and then slid close beside him. Sometimes if necessary, I would glide slowly beside a boat, then turn my steering wheel hard starboard, and then reverse my throttle hard. By doing so the combination of the boat moving forward and what I did, caused the boat to get sucked to the right, tightly putting my bumpers up against his port side. I then would put the engine in neutral, and cleat one black rope to their cleat midway.

"Yes sir, how can I help you?" I noticed his fishing pole in his hand had a lot of line out and was very high up in a tree on the shoreline.

"I had a pelican take my bait, and it flew way up there in the top of that tree!"

Laughing I said, "Yes sir, we all have had that happen. You want me to try to get it?"

"Yes, please do!" he said laughing also.

No doubt he would have tried himself had I not been there but was perhaps nervous at my presence. I stepped onto his boat and took the fishing pole. Simple things like this with many people watching can be spooky. We are supposed to be the experts at everything in the outdoors, and yet we can fall and make fools of ourselves like everyone else. I've always dealt with this by being careful, being myself, and being honest with people. I stayed on the bottom deck of the boat and gently reeled and jerked the pole repeatedly until the pelican scrambled outward from the tree and on the edge of a branch. I was hoping to pull the hook free, but instead I got a live pelican kite. I slowly reeled the bird in with a lot of loud chuckles behind me. The bird flew hard against me back and forth like a kite. I finally got it in and grabbed the large bird with one arm pinning its wings closed. It snapped hard at my face and I had to turn my head until I asked the fisherman to grab and keep its mouth shut. With the help of the fisherman and pliers, the hook was removed and the bird was freed with surrounding cheers. I was smeared with bird crap now, and my sunglasses were knocked off. I had to go to a marina restroom to clean myself up!

~

ONE DAY I was heading inbound from several miles offshore and was cruising about 40 mph in calm seas.

After I had checked a boat and was Idling away, a black cormorant bird landed on my remote spotlight on the bow of my patrol boat. I now still had it on my spotlight while cruising. I chuckled as it leaned into the wind, but then stopped in dismay as it spread its wings wide to dry and then crap all over my bow.

"Ok bird, try this for size," I said aloud to myself. I slowly increased my speed to fifty and slowly zig and zagged. It stayed on while leaning into the wind with its head down low! I smiled in admiration and then started to move my spotlight back and forth with the control next to my steering wheel. This caused the bird to rotate back and forth 180 degrees. It stayed on. I wished I had a camera beside me that day. I continued inbound towards the channel, passing other boaters who were smiling and pointing at the crazy bird rotating with its wings out wide on a moving patrol boat spotlight, while I was still cruising! It took a while, but after crapping again it finally took off.

～

DURING MY FIRST year in Crystal River, I noticed on many weekends a strange sight. An older man in Jon Boat about 18' would routinely head out Crystal River, to Shell Island. The island was about seven miles out and was near the mouth of the river entering the Gulf of Mexico. What made it amazing was whether he was moving fast or slow, two mallard ducks would follow him staying within ten feet of the boat. Sometimes I would see the ducks riding on the boat, instead of flying close beside it while cruising. More incredible, he always had a large black lab dog on the boat. So the ducks were always flying beside the boat, or sitting beside the dog! It was a very stop-and-point spectacle. Investigation revealed as we say, that the operator was a local artist and had his own gallery. I talked with him one day and only remember that he said he raised the ducks since chicks, and this is what they did almost every weekend. I don't think he would mind revealing his name was Mayo. It was over twenty years ago.

5

VESSELS HAVE NO BRAKES

Driving a car, truck, or motorcycle nowadays is probably the most dangerous thing we do every day. When a military policeman in Germany, I saw a lot of death and injury involving U.S military soldiers and their families in car accidents. Most occurred on the autobahn which had no speed limit and most often alcohol related. Even though off base, we had the authority and requirement to respond, help, and charge, based on the UCMJ. (Uniform Code of Military Justice).

Later in life as a Florida State Marine Patrol Officer, I also did this with vessels of all kinds, recreational and commercial for twenty-six years. We respond to help, enforce laws, and record all the information for court and statistic purposes. Many used our reports for insurance or civil lawsuit purposes. All our reports are assigned a complaint number, which I highly recommend the public ask for individually from the assigned officer. This can be used later to request a copy of the report, or status of an accident, complaint, title request, etc.

Vessels obviously have no brakes. Additionally, there are no stop signs, no speed limits offshore, no boat driver's license, no turn signals, no seat belts, and you are surrounded by water. Alcohol is also allowed by adults, but operators cannot be .08% or more. There are also water currents, wakes, steel channel markers, and other crazy operators, water skiers, etc.. zig-zagging back and forth coming at you! All the while sweat, salt spray, suntan lotion, bug spray, wind, and sun, are in your eyes as you are drinking a beer and crashing into wakes. A boat in nature is freedom and incredible, but can also ruin lives if not careful.

"Two thirty-one Crystal River," I said keying my mic. "

"231 go ahead," said dispatch...."I am 10-8 for the day" I advised.

"10-4, 231, ... be 10-51 to Yankeetown, reference a signal 4 fatality."

I replied, "10-26, is my vessel needed?"

"That's 10-54, Coast Guard, the SO and investigation are already on the scene"

"10-26. 10-51," I said, closing and putting up my mic. Normally I would have been called out early and would have run code with my vessel in tow. We are subject to call 24/7, unless on leave or sick. Often we are the last to be notified, as most boat accident calls by the public contact the U.S Coast Guard first with their VHF radio channel 16. The Coast Guard then will call our dispatch by phone with the information. I didn't run code except briefly and carefully blue lighted through a quiet intersection without a siren.

When I arrived along the Withlacoochee River river bank, I noticed small groups of people in the drizzling rain here and there. It was Easter or close to it I remember, also a very dreary and sad morning. Our Marine Patrol Investigator for that area walked up to me and we shook hands. He was recently single, dark-haired, a body-builder, and about six years older than I. The ladies loved him I had heard.

"Hey dude, good morning!" he said quietly crunching my hand and making my eyes water...

"Back at you! What's the scoop?"

"Well, this happened earlier... Three young adult males were hydro sliding early in that 18' boat tied up over there, he said pointing to it. I've already gotten statements and pics, just waiting for the S.O dive team to find the body. Apparently, one passenger lost his hat and when they swung around to retrieve it he fell overboard trying to grab it. He never came up, and you know how dark the water is and also of the tidal current... I'm guessing he also hit the prop... Additionally, alcohol was involved."

It is illegal to bow ride on a boat while moving. We will warn or cite the violation under "Careless Operation" as a catch-all. This is done because of so many accidents of people getting hit by the prop if they fall. A meat grinder we call it. Even if a boat is going idle speed and a person falls off the bow, he or she most likely will connect with the churning prop underwater. An operator's reaction time cannot possibly prevent this. While this was not a bow riding accident, it shows the danger of hitting the boat or prop.

We turned and each stood beside each other in the drizzle, surveying the sadness around us and awaiting the S.O dive team with their vessel in front of us, doing their dangerous job in dark moving water.

"Dude, check this out," he said quietly beside me. He proceeded to tell me about an obscene encounter he had with a woman. When he finished the story he looked hard at me, almost demanding I smirked. I could not help myself and smiled back. I nervously glanced around at the possibility of others approaching, while listening further...

The first time I had encountered this, to my surprise, was as a Military Policeman in Germany. I discovered over my L.E career of a total of 29yrs, that some officers and public even though caring and good people, will joke pervasively during a human tragedy. This I discovered was a coping mechanism, to relieve harsh reality and severe stress. My wife and daughter being an R.N, have seen similarities in their occupation.

I recall also one night at about 2 AM (0200hrs) in Germany, a drunk German woman wanted to commit suicide and quickly laid down in front of a vehicle just past a small hill in the rain. That vehicle ended up being a marked Military Police Van, which ran right over her. During the investigation by the German Police, the victim's friends at the scene confirmed what happened. My roommate, friend, brother Officer on patrol with me responded and arrived soon after. While she was being attended to, we helped block traffic as the suicidal woman screamed horribly in agony. As this was going on, my partner (we were only 19 years of age) proceeded to chuckle and comment on the woman "pissing on herself." I shook my head and grimaced. Had I not known how he would have done anything to help people, I would have knocked him out in private. That same partner in Germany later became an Officer in rank and was in the first Gulf War. He sustained some hearing loss and described grown men crying and screaming over the incessant bombing that took place. I still have the post-card he sent from Operation Desert Storm. Sometimes, people will do anything from going crazy.

The tall Marine Patrol Investigator my senior, continued with his quiet joking until the body bag in the front of us was pushed up into the boat by divers, and then pulled in by the boat passengers very respectfully. The groups of people on the river bank suddenly spread out and became deathly quiet... until a scream exploded out. All noticed a woman fall to her knees in the rain, and shake with agony. Her screams continued from utter despair. It raised the hair on my head. During this time it seemed the world stopped spinning for a second. Men I've noticed will grit their teeth, close their eyes, and punch anything near them repeatedly, not giving a damn about the physical pain. A woman however is more vocal, and you can hear the complete anguish, horror, and disbelief, as a part of her soul is broken into a million pieces.

You think I'm being overly dramatic for the book

maybe? I assure you I'm not even close. Imagine seeing for yourself as many have, after waiting for hours, and then suddenly seeing your child, spouse, or family's lifeless body. Not just pretend to think about it, but truly think about it for real. You will never see their smiling face again. Sometimes it seems, that the reality of a situation isn't fully realized until you see the reaction of a loved one. You then will know how that life is now gone and will affect many others' lives forever and how that person was truly loved. I have been involved in many successful rescues, one of which became personal and will describe how later. I remember bringing a couple of rescued men back to their home in Kings Bay, after having been reported missing and rescued many hours later from offshore. While returning them they huddled wet in a blanket and put on a brave face. However, when I pulled up to the dock and their loved ones came running to them crying loudly in relief, the rescued men cried with them. It isn't until you see the other person's reaction, that you fully react yourself. This is why it is so important to look calmly at a victim, and tell them they will be OK with confidence. That alone may calm them, as they are using your face as a mirror.

When the earth began spinning again the Investigator turned towards me, "That's a wrap dude, I won't need you" he said quietly. I nodded my goodbye and solemnly walked away. I observed the devastated woman again about 20 yards away still on her knees shaking. Her family and friends had made a protective cocoon over her in the rain, all gripping each other tightly. Knowing that nothing on God's green earth was going to help that devastated woman, except time....and hopefully her faith. I walked on in the increasing rain.

"230 Crystal River, "I said in my mic back in the patrol car.

"Go ahead 230."

"I'm 10-98. The body has been recovered by the S.O. dive team. Investigations released me. Back 10-8."

I went back on patrol and knew as various times before, I would have to complete my shift with a fake smile to the public while answering their daily legal questions. I believe with every fiber of my being that the good souls of the deceased are in an indescribable beautiful place. The living of course has to continue on, learning their required lessons. The screaming and pounding of the earth is an important step toward the grieving process. I surmised as I drove away, that this is a lesson to cherish all life and not be careless with your own.

It was revealed later, that the prop (engine propeller), did indeed make contact with the victim's forehead, apparently killing him instantly. My sincere condolences to that family, as well as many others who lost family to the sea. Some never being found at all.

As with any police officer I can go on forever about accidents, many relating to alcohol, inattention, carelessness, reckless, bad judgment, mechanical, inexperience, nighttime, storms, and sometimes just plain unlucky. I have been involved in boat mishaps also, which I will cover in my "Blunders" chapter.

One day a jet ski got hit by a large motorboat in

Crystal River on a holiday weekend, pushing the jet ski operator and jet ski upside down into the water. The operator popped up with no injuries at all. His jet ski however, actually had deep prop marks over the bottom! Lucky!

I remember also how a couple of older guys were anchored up and fishing in the Gulf in a small boat when a large commercial shrimp boat heading out went straight at them. It was a clear afternoon. The older guys jumped up frantically and blew a whistle to no avail. They ended up leaping over the side just in time to avoid the crash. The shrimp boat operator was alone and was working on something in the back, as the boat continued out. After the crash, he did jump overboard to help the older fishermen. It was lucky they did not get killed!

~

LASTLY, for this chapter anyway, I'll mention how Sea Tow one day was towing in a good 20' or better vessel into Crystal River. They tow at slow speeds, are marked in bright yellow, and have flashing yellow lights. Additionally, at the time it was daytime and it was towing in a marked Manatee slow zone. Coming up swiftly behind that Sea Tow at the same time, was an older married couple who decided to look at an osprey on top of a manatee sign. The osprey birds frequently do this and have hatch-lings on them year after year. I've even had to remove a little of the nests, so people can clearly see the sign.

The older couple's vessel then proceeded to crash into

the towed vessel, went over its stern, hit the back of the seat which sat the owner, and swung over to the starboard side back into the water. This was again in broad daylight and in a well-marked manatee slow zone. Luckily, the man sitting in the seat being towed was only grazed hard, and amazingly not really injured other than bad bruising to his right side and upper buttocks, which I later took pictures of in his yard for evidence. There was also, as you can imagine, a lot of damage to the boats. I cited the subject vessel for "Careless Operation-Failure to Keep a Proper Lookout." This was only an infraction. There were no other alcohol, serious bodily injury, safety equipment or registration, or other violations. "Reckless Operation", which I did not charge them for, is criminal and usually requires a court appearance. The definition of it includes "willful and wanton". All elements of the crime have to be met, for an officer to make that charge. Otherwise, it will be thrown out. This is true for all crimes in America.

However, even an infraction coupled with our statements, pictures, etc. can be a big problem. Insurance is not required for a boat on state waters, at least not back then. Hence, people may sue for hospital and damage expenses. That's when our reports and testimony can be obtained and required in civil cases. A boat accident does require our response in most cases. Call the FWC or visit their website for any questions. Leaving a scene of an accident, failure to provide help, failing to report to L.E, etc. are serious crimes. I always recommend being slow and careful of course, but to avoid civil problems get the complaint number from the officer, and try to work it out with the other party if plausible. If you do exchange information and/or money to settle small damage, I would do it with witnesses and a notary. This does "not" exempt you from the reporting requirements. Violations may still be cited, based on the total evidence. The officer legally is required to do this, even though having not actually seen the accident occur but by evidence only.

6

THE JOKER

The joker as I'll call him for the book, was a Florida Marine Patrol Investigator. He is a silver tongue and silver hair type A personality that can sell ice to Eskimos and talk a coon out of a tree. He talks fast and is usually laughing in every sentence; generally with jokes at your expense. You cannot however stop yourself from laughing, due to his personality and watching him laugh hysterically at you. If you ever have enough of him, and tell him to go fly a kite so to speak, his favorite response is "So, what are trying to say Kam?" He says this with a smirk while squinting at you and then laughs hysterically at your insult toward him. It's a no-win situation. His philosophy in life is "It's better to get forgiveness than permission." Also,"It's water off a ducks back!"

One day the Joker, the Italian (Big boned family man officer, friendly, patrolled the water a lot like me, affectionately called by some "River Daddy") and myself were talking together. The Joker finished up by saying, "I almost unsnapped!" (Meaning jokingly, he almost unsnapped and drew his gun.)

The Italian looking at the Joker who was laughing hysterically at one of his own jokes, suddenly and loudly yelled at the joker, **"Let me see your balls! Let me see your balls! You must have the biggest balls this side of Texas! Your balls have to be made of brass!! Let me see your damn balls.**

After a short quiet pause, the Joker and myself started laughing so hard, it was hard to breathe. The Italian on another occasion mentioned to me and the joker stating "I know how to tell when he is lying" he said pointing to the joker.

"How?" I asked.

"Simple, it's when his lips are moving.

We all laughed. The Italians' favorite saying in conflict was "I should have zigged instead of zagged!" The Italian himself got me one day in Kings Bay. I had a fancy writing pen I personally had bought that fell over in about three feet of water. He encouraged me to slip over and dive for it as no one was around at the moment. I did so, and when I stood up in the water he had moved the boat away laughing. He even took a picture. (Gotta have fun when you can I guess.)

I had heard from an officer, that one time the Joker had actually paid for a local newspaper article advertising another officer's patrol boat for sale! That Officer was flooded with calls to buy it until he called the newspaper and discovered who the culprit was! My first encounter with a Joker prank, was when I tiredly pulled my patrol boat up to the boat ramp at the end of my shift. It was dark and I was ready to back my trailer down, load up my boat and gear, rinse off everything, fill up with gas, and head home. I walked up to my black and gray Crown Victoria patrol car with the boat trailer attached and happily noted that although other trailers were present, I was the only one there and thus didn't have to answer questions, or wait in line. I opened the door and sat starting to relax from the day.

When I put the key in the ignition and started it, all hell broke loose! My windshield wipers started beating furiously back and forth, the hazards lights came on, the take down lights front and back came on, my very bright blue lights turned on, my siren began blasting, the radio was even blasting. My heart jumped in my throat! I froze for a second being totally caught off guard! I scrambled and fumbled in the dark car to shut it all off, as the blues lights illuminated brightly in the dark and the siren screamed in the shattered silence! I discovered later the joker liked to do this, using a spare key for the vehicle we all had in a known location for emergencies. This was possible the way things were back then.

The Joker got me again at the boat ramp years later, not to mention other pranks. I had finished a day of water patrol and had just pulled my boat out of the water. I then got out and went to the back of the boat. I lowered the engine and put the engine brackets in place. I put the boat strap on and unloaded my gear. I did this there as long as I wasn't blocking anybody. I was quick anyway from years of repetition. Suddenly, as I bent down carefully under the 225 hp outboard engine to pull the plug out, the boat started to move forward! The boat ramp there was very close to high way 19 and had a lot of back and forth traffic. I had left my car engine running but had parked it for sure with the emergency break on, so I thought. With my heart beating out of my chest, I tore around the 21 foot boat and ran towards the patrol car door which was open! The car was getting close to entering the high way! I literately envisioned a crash, hurting people, and getting fired in shame! As I got to the open door and was ready to leap in, I saw the Joker hunched over low in the seat in his civilian clothes, with both hands on the steering wheel, and just now stepping hard on the brake. As he saw my scared pale face, his face got red, and he started laughing hysterically! The more I relayed my fear and the more I scolded, the more he laughed. Damn Joker!

∼

THE JOKER MANEUVERED HIS ASSIGNED 21' fast Answer Marine patrol boat expertly in the calm Gulf of Mexico. Like I did also, he maneuvered it towards his intended target, keeping the marked Marine Patrol side from its view and then bombing towards the target from offshore of it at the last minute. (Making sure to always go parallel of the target, in case of engine stall.) Doing this hopefully didn't alert the occupants until the last moment that we were law. This hopefully prevents possible illegal fish from being tossed overboard. I have however made fish cases even when dumped. I still wrote them a ticket because either the illegal fish I witnessed tossed over were dead and I was able to retrieve them, or based on what I saw and what they stated to me. I could still cite them for not "Failure to immediately return saltwater products and unharmed to the water." Yes, that is a real charge. All fish violations by the way are criminal misdemeanors, although some judges allow for a mail in fine instead of a mandatory court appearance as some counties require. So please get some free regulations or take a fast picture and carefully return it to the water. Putting the fish in the bucket or cooler, means your "intention to keep."

As we pulled up to the 16' skiff with one male occupant, I threw out the black bumpers. I then tied our boat to his as the Joker began talking.

"Good afternoon captain. I'm Officer "Joker"(Fiction name), and this is Officer Johnson of the Florida Marine Patrol. May we see your fishing license and boat registration please?

As the Joker was talking, I noticed the man was nervous, and sitting down with a towel across his lap. I looked around scanning for possible hidden areas where illegal fish can be hidden. We can search everywhere that is "realistic" for saltwater products. Obviously, we can't search a woman's purse for a Grouper, unless she gives permission, LOL. I also glanced at his registration numbers and decal on the port side we were tied to, for possible improper display, expiration, spacing, and contrasting color. I remember one time, I saw a boater display his entire 12-character hull identification number as a boat registration number, which looked really funny on both sides of his bow. We educate a lot, and more often than not correct a violation with a verbal or written warning unless it's been recorded that you have already been warned for that before.

At the Joker's question, the man stayed sitting and reached out to the stern of the smaller skiff and grabbed a plastic container containing his paperwork.

"Any luck with catching any fish?" the Joker asked while also looking around for a bucket or compartment.

"Nawww, just small stuff so far " he replied as he handed over his paperwork.

The Joker took the paperwork with his left hand, as we always try to keep our gun hand free. The Joker smiled suddenly with his silver hair glistening in the sun. He casually removed his gold-rimmed Ray-Ban sunglasses to see better. He then pointed at the man's crotch area. Something about twelve inches long was flopping around under the towel between his legs!

"Is that a fish sir, or are you just happy to see me?"

I noticed it too of course and reached out to pull the towel away. The man's face turned beet red as the still alive undersized spotted sea-trout was revealed. He got a $150.00 misdemeanor fine that he could mail-in or contest in court. Nowadays it's over $300.00 per violation, depending on which county you are in. Violations like the above were common, but the Joker's statement and humor was one of a kind. I could go on and on about the Joker but will conclude with only a couple more.

One time the Joker got a hold of a life-sized pizza humanoid used for advertising and set it up to look like it was operating a rental pontoon boat at a marina owned by a Marine Patrol Reserve Officer. In the morning many saw it and laughed. The pontoon was in the water tied to the marina dock.

~

ANOTHER TIME, I was riding with the Joker in town in a rain storm and he elected to run in and drop off his insurance bill with his handheld radio. As an Investigator, he got to wear plain clothes when desired. After waiting forever for him I got disgusted and went in to get him. Inside he was joking around with others and an employee there offered me some cookies and coffee. I sheepishly agreed. I swallowed a couple of bites, then froze! The Joker and others there suddenly stopped talking and stared at me. They began to laugh hysterically as I spit out sloppily into a trash can. All the moisture in my mouth dried up! I could hardly talk! They had apparently put a spice like Alum or something that caused this. Damn Joker!

I was able to get revenge a few times with the Joker. Besides doing the horn, light, and siren key start thing to him, I dragged a huge floating log near the ramp area one night and put it under his and the Italian's patrol car to block them! My shift on a Holiday weekend ended earlier than theirs, around midnight. They may have been trying for more overtime. When I pulled my boat out nobody was around. It took everything I had to drag that heavy water-soaked 10' long log out of the water and shove it under their parked side-by-side patrol cars. It hurt my back, and I got dirty and sweaty doing it, but I smirked in the dark all the same.

After I got home and cleaned up I got into bed with my handheld radio beside me. I had the officer talk around ch.3 scanning as always. As my wife questioned my anticipated stupid giggling self laying in bed at 1 am, I was indeed rewarded.

"Heyyyyyyyyy! Somebody put a huge log under our patrol cars!" The Italian apparently had arrived first and was relaying the problem to the Joker on the talk around officer channel. (Low band back then)

"What! Are you serious?" the Joker replied back.

"Yes I'm serious! The log is huge, and I'm going to need help!!" The Italian sounded stressed and out of breath.

I heard no more radio chatter from them for several minutes and so shut my radio off. I giggled snorted and chuckled to myself while laying in bed for a good ten minutes before I fell asleep. To this day I'm not sure If I ever told them who did it. (I know I know, blocking emergency vehicles is not to bright, but it had gotten very quiet at the late hour and it was soooo funny!)

Lastly, I filled out a warning ticket on the Joker and framed it in a glass picture frame. I filled in the blanks with things like "Pain in the butt violations." On the day of the Joker's retirement, I got up early and went lights and siren in front of his house, hopefully waking him up. I left the warning ticket for his present!

(The Joker actually was an excellent Investigator. Thanks for all the memories Joker!)

7

OUI (OPERATING UNDER THE INFLUENCE) CHASE

U nlike in a motor vehicle on land, in Florida it is actually legal to drink alcoholic beverages if 21 years of age and operate a vessel. Naturally, you can't be .08% blood alcohol content or under the influence. If you are on a boat and operate unsafely while drinking, you will be asked to perform field sobriety tasks if stopped by an law enforcement officer. If you get arrested and refuse to blow on the intoxilyzer at the jail, you still will be charged as being "under the influence", instead of the charge being at or over the blood alcohol limit. Also, refusing to submit to the intoxilyzer is held against you in court and you will be additionally fined a civil penalty. This comes from "The Implied Consent Law" when you sign for your boat registration or driver's license. The evidence if you refuse to blow, then becomes your refusal, failing the sobriety tasks, documented observations of the arresting officer and the jail staff, odor, empty containers, video, pics, etc. If convicted of OUI or DUI, it is both considered in conjunction with each other-meaning an OUI and a DUI conviction in a year, is two of the same, a second offense. The penalties from a judge and statute will get stiffer and stiffer. Here is one of my more memorable OUI offenses on the upper Homosassa River.

"Marine Patrol, Marine Patrol on the Homosassa River!" I was in my marked 19' Pathfinder Marine Patrol boat with 225 Hp motor drifting in front of a marina. I had just used the restroom and gotten a cold drink. It was a very hot and humid over 90 degrees, typical Florida afternoon weekend. Kids were out of school and families were on vacation enjoying the clear cool spring water of the upper river, as well as coming to and from the connecting Gulf of Mexico.

"Marine Patrol on the Homosassa River!" The urgent voice was emitting from my VHF radio on channel 16, which is reserved for emergencies and hailing only. If you didn't have an emergency and were jabbering away on CH 16, the U.S Coast Guard from Yankeetown would give you a stern "be advised" speech basically telling you to switch to another channel or else.

I opened my console compartment protecting my VHF radio from salt spray and grabbed the mic. "Marine Patrol on the Homosassa River go ahead over!"

"Marine Patrol! A fast red speed boat is blowing the idle zone in the springs and almost hit us! It's waking everybody and is speeding down the river!"

"10-4 Captain I'm headed that way, over."

I threw the mic back in the compartment and put the motor in forwarding gear. I slowly maneuvered around another boat and then around a tiny Island in the idle zone. I slowly moved up the river with a clear view. As I was already in the upper seven-mile-long river I expected the speeding red boat any second now. The river was only about 40 yards wide where I was. Sure enough, here it came! The bright red "Terminator" bass boat was hauling butt directly towards me. It had two white adult passengers and the boat was throwing a high rooster tail of water with a large roaring outboard motor toward me. I broadsided my boat so they could see its markings and turned on my bright flashing blue lights. Instead of stopping, it did a sharp U-turn throwing a huge wake, and screamed away in the opposite direction. I punched my throttle forward and gave chase. While chasing the boat with lights and siren I wanted to call it in to dispatch but was too intent on the chase and was carefully avoiding other recreational boaters. I had, of course, one hand on the steering wheel and the other on the throttle to make constant adjustments. Everybody in the area was watching the high-speed chase like it was on a Hollywood movie set. My Pathfinder was fairly light and was one the fastest patrol vessel I ever had. It was also low in the water line like the bass boat I was chasing.

Over time, chases became more and more restrictive in policy for public safety, but in this case, I felt easily justified as it was a definite threat to public safety, even before I began chasing it. Time seems to slow in stressful times but the chase was probably only a couple of minutes of zig-zagging at high speed up and down the upper river. I kept a safe distance, and not knowing what to expect my heart was pounding. It finally quickly slowed and semi-crashed against a long wooded private dock on the North side of the river. Thank God it didn't go all the up the river where people swim in the headwater spring!

I witnessed the operator scramble off the boat and stagger quickly away. The passenger stayed put and started to attempt to tie the boat to the dock. I slid up behind it and tied up also. I quickly reported the situation to my dispatch and requested a backup.

"Stay put!" I yelled and pointed at the passenger still in the boat. I had shut off the siren and pulled my boat key sticking it in my pocket. I also grabbed my handheld and hurriedly followed after the runaway operator. I had noted carefully the subject boat's registration and occupant's appearance. Both adults had shorts and shirts on and I didn't see any potential weapon. I jogged forward while hooking my radio to my belt and scanning ahead of me. I quickly got to the roadway which parallels the river closely. Not seeing anyone I walked slowly across the roadway looking around. I didn't feel the need to draw my gun.

"Officer!" a man yelled behind

I quickly turned around and saw a bystander back across the road near a house on the river. He was waving his arms back and forth waving me towards him. I quickly ran back across the street towards him. He was excited and out of breath. He lowered his voice.

"I saw the guy you were chasing. He tossed something small and crawled into the water over there.

He pointed to a tiny pond just past his house in a grassy area. Perhaps a low spot with rainwater. As we both looked my subject jumped up from the water who had been laying on his belly.

I yelled "stop, police!"

He then spastically ran away back towards the river and dove in! Giving chase I ran and jumped back into my patrol boat. I started it back up and quickly untied the one cleated rope while trying to keep an eye on the runaway subject swimming away and the still sitting passenger in the subject boat beside me.

"Stay here!" I advised him.

I then slowly motored down the river as I literally followed the swimming subject who was between my boat and the river bank. As I reported the info to dispatch I also noticed a lot of boaters and people were still watching in fascination. With my flashing blue lights still on I got ahead of the swimming subject and pulled alongside the next private dock. I secured to it quickly. I noticed the subject was tiring and wasn't watching me. I climbed up on the dock and kneeled down. The subject was swimming right towards me.

My dispatch during the chase had notified the Citrus County Sheriff's Dept. for backup, as no other Marine Patrol Officers were 10-8 at the time. We just say the "S.O". Unbeknown to me a deputy arrived by vehicle in the area and had seen my blue lights thru the trees by the roadway. He followed me along near the river. When I stopped he quickly got out and ran towards me being the pro he was. I leaned over the dock and reaching hard grabbed the subject by the hair! It was the only thing I could grab. He quickly stopped and stood up in about four feet of clear brackish water. When he stood up I lost grip of his hair but then was able to grab his arm. He began yelling and resisting, but I was younger and stronger then. I pulled hard and got him close to the dock. The deputy (bless him) quickly arrived and reached out also. It took both of us to pull the fighting dead weight of the subject out of the water and over the dock. We put him face down each having an arm and using an arm bar technique which uses non lethal pressure for compliance. The pain caused him to stop struggling, at which point I was able to fish out my handcuffs and handcuff him. I did a fast pat-down on him and we both stood him up to the cheering and clapping of the boaters behind us.

Those handcuffs of mine were made in America by Smith and Wesson. I have used them dozens of times. I still have them today for sentimental reasons. I had a spare pair which I turned in upon retirement. The Joker, no doubt, would have jokingly requested them for himself and his wife.

The deputy transported the subject away to the jail for me. I would arrive later to complete the many paged booking report, as well as my citations, OUI forms, refusal to blow form, etc. Not to mention a long "Offense Incident/Summary report." (If you don't see an officer on patrol it's because he is either in court, in training, or doing paperwork.)

I still had to secure my boat and deal with the subject boat. Its passenger was cooperative, had no warrants, and allegedly tried to stop his OUI friend. I took pictures and recorded his information, then permitted him to secure the subject boat to lessen my workload. Before leaving, I also searched the boat and the area for whatever small item the subject ditched, but I had no luck and needed to get to the jail. I suspected no doubt, it had been drugs. When I arrived at the jail later, a correctional officer quickly approached me smirking. "Are you Johnson?" he asked.

I answered "Yes"

He was holding a video camera and handed it to me laughing.

"You won't have to go to court on this one!

I played back the video he showed me. The subject had stripped himself down naked and was playing with himself. The correction officers also stated they had to pepper spray the subject twice to stop his combativeness. Additionally, he had blown snot on the jail nurse when she tried to look at him for injuries after they struggled with him.

I charged him with OUI, Felony Fleeing and Alluding, Resisting Arrest Without Violence, Failure to Submit to the Breathalyzer, and Violation of a Manatee Zone. It was lucky nobody was killed! The corrections officer was right, I didn't have to go to court on that one!

8

UNUSUAL NAMES

W riting non-fiction about others is a risk of course, even though again I am mainly using fictitious names, and being somewhat general. Also, as with all law enforcement deputies and reports, everything we do is public information except for juveniles. Lastly, in this huge world of ours, you can find the same name for almost everyone, regardless of its "uniqueness." If you don't believe it, try searching your name online. So yes, the names in this chapter are all real!

"Lightning Rod" (my nickname for him because his house got hit by lightning) and I had parked our patrol car behind a building at a local marina. It was around 1:00 A.M., or 0100 hours as we say. We were working some rare overtime issued hours for resource protection. There are no "quotas" for us as the public sometimes thinks, but our supervisors and the bean counters in Tallahassee expect "activity". This justifies money issued and equipment etc.

"Activity" can be complaints worked, warnings, PR (public relations) functions, safety inspection forms, search and rescues, citations and arrests. Our "activity" is reviewed monthly, on holiday weekends, on special details, and annually by the supervisors. This is how we are judged and evaluated mostly.

We stood in the dark talking quietly, hoping for a boat to come in soon for us to check. We had been there since midnight. A large boat could be heard in the distance chugging noisily up the windy river, upwards from the entrance of the Gulf many miles away. The noise indicated it was diesel powered, most likely a commercial boat. (A funny word diesel, with the word "die" in it.) We waited patiently in the dark until the large commercial vessel came into view and pulled noisily into its designated boat slip. The diesel fumes emitted strongly to our noses. We stayed hidden, observing everything. It appeared there was only one white adult male on the boat and no apparent lookouts or others waiting on him. Many commercial vessels do a variety of things, including shrimping, crabbing, reef fish, just to name a few. All of which require commercial markings, commercial safety equipment, saltwater product licenses, restricted species endorsement, live wells, turtle excluding devices, trawl requirements, and on and on. It all depends on seasons, the location, and what they are targeting and are in possession of. The public has no idea about the huge volume of information we had to know. Some commercial fishermen complained about trying to remember all the requirements, but I would rebuke them.

"All you have to know is the one thing you are doing, blue crabbing, etc. We have to know it all! You guys make a living daily on that one thing... year after year."

It should be noted that most commercial fishermen are honest hard working people with families. They work long hours and have dangerous jobs. Many have assisted in search and rescues. Even towing the sometimes stranded public. I always had high respect for most of them. They provide America with tasty seafood for the rest of us to enjoy, despite their difficult and hazardous labor.

In the dark, Lightning Rod and I slid up beside the boat captain tying up his last line to the dock.

"Good evening Captain, Fish and Wildlife Commission!" Rod declared loudly over the engine noise as he got closer.

Both of us snapped on our flashlights even though there was some light shed from the Marina lights. The boat captain almost had a heart attack as he obviously was startled and shocked at our appearance. He had been blinded by the deck lights he just turned on recently. (I always did love sneaking up on people on the job. It was a challenge and necessary to make good cases.

"Please shut your engine off captain" Rod continued. The captain complied and retrieved the boat registration we asked for. As the boat was docked and we were working on a resource detail we weren't interested in safety equipment. We did check his saltwater products license also since he had some legal shrimp onboard.

"Do you have any other saltwater products anywhere else on this boat?" I asked.

I learned to ask this because people will get nervous at the question, and sometimes retrieve fish from the darnedest unexpected places. I have heard from other officers even that they found duck meat stuffed in portable fuel tanks and lobster stuffed in dive tanks down south in the Keys, all with hidden compartments.

"Nawwww, that's it." he replied.

Rod and I continued to open hatches and look around.

"What's in that bag?!" Rod asked suddenly.

He had opened up a hatch, bent down, and looked far back into it with his flashlight.

"Uhhhhhhhhh, that's just some ol Grouper Fillets" he replied sheepishly.

While Rod held the flashlight and watched the captain I bent down low and reached in deep stretching my arm out grabbing and pulling out the large plastic bag stuffed with Grouper fillets. There were many, most likely undersized. All regulated fish have to be landed in whole condition, meaning the head and tail have to be attached and the skin still on. The fish can be gutted though. This is necessary to give us a chance to measure it and also to check for season violations. If the identity can't be determined, we can seize the product and have it analyzed through FDLE submission. FDLE can do many things, even things like determining if a light filament was on or off during a crash.

"I thought you said there was nothing else!?" Rod questioned sternly.

The subject just shrugged.

My older senior partner had found the violation, but it was my turn to write. When Officers hook up, it was common to take turns writing the violation. This gives both Officers "activity" to record on their monthly logs. The case was a good one, and so I looked guiltily towards Rod, who then gave me a go ahead nod to write the citation. I could have also charged him with "Interfering with a Law Enforcement Officer" for lying to us. However, I elected to just make it a mandatory court appearance and also describe him lying on the citation for the Judge to see.

I grabbed my large resource citation book in its metal cover and retrieved the subject's driver's license. Each citation had its individual number at the top. Each citation book and its numbers are signed for by the officer. Before holiday weekends, we always had to pick up extra citation books, inspection forms, suntan lotion, etc.. from the district office in anticipation of the long hot humid, and busy 12 hour shift days to come. (I always prayed and did a rain dance before the weekend started. LOL).

I scrutinized the driver's license and boat registration with my tired eyes and completed the citation and property receipt for the fish. Rod kept watch. I then had the subject sign the citation. The mandatory signing is not an admission of guilt, but an acknowledgment of the charge and requirement of its instructions. Failure to do so, even an infraction possibly, results in your physical arrest. A physical arrest is always an option if the subject is from out of the area, a flight risk, or non-compliant.

"Press down, five copies" I advised as he signed. I then detached his copy and handed it to him saying, "Ok Mr. Ahole, you must appear on that court date."

Rod and the subject's eyes about popped out!

The subject looked up with a stern face.

"Uhhhh, that's pronounced "Ahhhh Ho!"

I'm not kidding, his last name was Aho! In my defense I was tired. I did apologize! (I'd be a liar though if I said Rod and I didn't laugh on the way home).

Years later working with Lightning Rod, we had a week of just working in plain clothes at various land fishing sites, like boat ramps or the "Red Fish Hole". I had named it that years earlier and it stuck. It was a trail off Fort Island Trail that led to the backwaters of Salt River. We would hide off the trail and stop people day and evening who were walking back to their car with buckets of fish. We had made so many fish cases during that week at the Red Fish Hole, we started sticking sticks in the ground every time we wrote a misdemeanor fish ticket to keep track for fun. We accumulated a lot of sticks!

One day I went there by myself and stood off the trail at our usual spot. I could see a long way down the trail, which allowed me to see people coming with possible fish caught. Sometimes they had lookouts, but I was wise to that. I suddenly noticed the grass and bushes were flattened around me. I was standing under a tree for shade. After looking around more closely, I noticed a huge alligator cabled to the tree! It had obviously thrashed around and spun, causing it to choke itself to death. It was only about a day old! Some angry customers had tried to get us with an alligator! I later contacted the Buffer Preserve Park office which managed the property, and they removed it. It must have been at least nine feet long and was illegally caught, of course. God only knows how alive!

∾

ONE LATE AFTERNOON ON A SUNDAY, I drove to our local FWC office near the Florida Barge Canal. It was my Friday and I needed to turn in my paperwork before I headed home. On nights and weekends, officers used the office by way of an alarm code; it was otherwise closed to the public at that time frame. Whenever I went to the office I most often did a quick detour and checked the nearby boat ramp for "customers". The ramp was right next to the office, which the public and ourselves used often to patrol that area, which went straight to the Gulf of Mexico.

When I pulled into the boat ramp I got lucky, a good-sized motorboat with fishing poles hanging out of it had just been pulled out. The boat was dripping wet, and two young white adult males were in the process of unloading the boat. After identifying myself I checked their cooler. There were several fish violations and so I ended up having to write a ticket. As I commonly did, I gave them the option of someone taking responsibility for the violation and receiving the ticket. Technically I could cite both of them for being in possession of illegal fish. The boat captain/boat owner elected to take responsibility and receive the citation. The citation book can list several violations; I elected to cite two of the violations and give written warnings for the other two. Upon receiving his driver's license I was immediately surprised! I looked carefully at the driver's license again and then did a double take at the subject.

"Your name is Kam Johnson?" I asked him with a look of incredibility! He immediately took it the wrong way.

"Oh sure, write me a fu@#$%^ ticket and make fun of my name!"

I shook my head and couldn't help a smile.

"No it's not that, it's just that we have the same name!"

"What!" he said with surprise. "No fu@#$%^ way!"

"I'm serious!" I put down the ticket book and showed him my badge and picture ID to him and also the now attentive passenger who had been finishing loading the boat.

"Wow! Well now you can't write me a fu@#$%^ ticket! We have the same fu@#$%^ name!"

Even though he was wound up and cussing profusely in his shirtless tattooed body self, I felt no threat from him. In fact, I couldn't help but to smile at the irony of it all. Picking up my ticket book again I continued. Sorry Kam, I'm actually giving you a break on a couple of them, and I could have written both of you. Also, you are right next to the FWC office after all!"

I wished the heck I had kept a copy of that ticket! It would have been funny to show others years later. I would have blocked his personal info of course.

My mom saw the name "Cam" in a book, and my parents liked it but changed it to "Kam". In school, it was unusual at the time and I got made fun of sometimes.

Over the years especially when in the Army I have been nick named Kambo, Camelot, Camcorder, and Camshaft. Now many decades later, it has actually become somewhat popular. There are many "Kams" now, even in my county! Go figure.....

~

I PUNCHED my heavy 21 foot Mako patrol boat with its 225 HP Johnson motor to its limit. The Mako boat was great to slug through storms and rough seas, but I had to be creative to go in shallow water or to try to catch other boaters. Sometimes with that particular boat, I wouldn't turn my blue lights on a violator until I saw it slowing down for a Manatee Zone. I didn't want the embarrassment of not being able to catch it with others watching. The boat would be a great fishing boat though.

I was inbound from the Gulf and headed towards the Salt River shortcut to get into Crystal River and head home. While en route, I noticed a small fishing boat off Fort Island Beach. It was in about two and a half feet of water it looked like and the tide was coming in. I decided to go for it and began to zig and zag the sand bars to get to the boat. I had seen one adult male passenger fishing in it. My zig zagging helped get some sea grass off my prop, and I had trimmed my prop up to the limit. My engine was screaming its max, as I was in shallow water and wanted to skim over it as best I could. As I slowed I trimmed up my motor a little more knowing the boat would sink down lower and would be skimming the bottom. There were times while idling slowly in shallow water, I had to stand in the front bow area to use my weight and help the boat from grounding while still in gear and moving forward. I threw my black bumpers out and tied my one black rope to his middle cleat.

"Good afternoon captain, I'm Officer Johnson of the Florida Marine Patrol. May I see your fishing license and boat registration please?"

He complied and stated, "I never saw such a large boat in this shallow water, how do you do it?"

"A lot of practice sir!"

(I didn't tell him the time when I had just been reassigned here and got stuck so bad coming out of Salt River, I had to wait two hours for the tide to fully come in before I could power out. While waiting, I had a local commercial blue crab fisherman come up to me in his skiff boat and asked if I needed help while smiling behind his crinkled eyes. I gave my "No thanks" and he left. He probably went to the fish house after and laughed his butt off with his buddies.)

"I'm sorry sir, your fishing license is very expired. I'll give you a warning for your boat registration numbers and missing letters but will have to give you a mail-in fine for the expired license. May I have your driver's license please?"

"I'm sorry, I don't have it with me. I locked it up in my car."

"That's ok sir. Just give me your full name and DOB and I'll run it through dispatch."

"Uhhhh, ok. It's Homer --- Simpson.

I tried not to smile but he saw right thru me.

"I know I know, I get that a lot!" he stated.

I continued with dispatch, Keith Miritello who was our long-time local dispatch during the day. He intelligently fielded probably a hundred questions a day from the public. I saw a black and white photo of Keith's dad one time guarding Frank Sinatra! His dad had been a bodyguard!

"I need a 10-27 check. First name Homer. Middle ---. Last name Simpson. Dob

I could audibly hear Keith chuckle over the radio before giving me the information. Additionally, the gentleman was over fifty, white, and balding. He then volunteered his occupation, knowing what was on my mind.

"And yes, I do work at the power plant!"

"I swear to GOD! You can't make this stuff up! He was a good sport, and I pray if he ever reads this he won't be offended. He would be over 80 years of age now.

~

ONE DAY while working on the Hurricane Andrew detail, another officer and I broke up one of many fights. The fights were usually only yelling and swearing due to cutting in line. We were guarding a FEMA trailer that had their employees giving out money in a rough area just outside the destroyed Homestead area. It was very hot and humid outside, and with long lines of people who sadly lost everything.

During the loud argument between two adult men, we heard "Get back in line mudda fuc#@r!" We of course broke it up and settled it quickly.

There were four of us, two inside the trailer and two outside. We rotated during the 12hrs shifts and sometimes carried shotguns. The trailer contained we heard at least a quarter of a million dollars in cash. There were no alarms as there was no power and everything around was completely destroyed by the hurricane.

That evening when the crowds left, Officer Chris Aoussat and I, played a game of checkers on a hand drawn board I had scratched out on paper during short breaks. We used coins for checkers. While two played checkers, the other two kept watch. We had time to do this on Sunday or night shift if all was quiet. After hearing that cussing earlier, we later thought it was hilarious. We started using it in private whenever it could be fitted in. We even changed our voices while saying it....

"Sooooooo, you want to challenge me in checkers Mudda Fuc#@r?"

"Oh yea, bring it on you Mudder Fuc#@r!"

It should be noted I was the oldest child and grew up with a Christian mom and went to Sunday school in a small country town in New England.

In those days soap was used for bad language.

My dad, while fixing the car and banging his knuckles would censor himself if us kids were around. "Son of a pup!" he would yell holding his injured hand and me ducking from a flying wrench.

Now, here I am twenty years later in Florida's 95-

degree humid weather while wearing a state law enforcement uniform throwing F- bombs around in a funny voice while snickering guiltily like an idiot.

We called politicians "Mudda Fuc#@rs! Supervisors Mudda Fu#@rs and even each other "Mudda Fuc#@rs.

One time during the day, a young creole child broke away from the line and wandered into the busy road behind the trailer. I had been watching and so managed to spastic-ally save him from a car slamming on his brakes and almost hitting him.

My adrenalin had kicked in and I saved his life.

My partner soon after came up to me and whispered loudly "Good Job Mudda Fuc#@r!!"

Lastly, with names, I always thought it was interesting that dog spelled backward is GOD (man's best friend). Also, the sun that is above us and gives all life resembles the "son" of man, that gave his life, and saved us all....

9

MY MISHAPS, MISTAKES, AND ACCIDENTS

I could describe other officers' mistakes and mishaps as well of course; such as an overturned Mako boat on highway 19, a battery falling on a foot breaking a toe, a boat popping off a trailer hitch and taking out a fence, a sunk airboat, on and on. However, due to concern over my safety from other brother officers (ha ha), I will only describe my mishaps. But this is worth repeating: the officer describing the unmarked patrol boat which popped off the hitch while traveling down Highway 19 had stated this, "When I looked to the left and saw my patrol boat getting ready to pass me, you couldn't have driven a tin penny nail up my ass!"

My Lt. (Lieutenant) advised, "Go ahead and get your camera, Kam. We should get a few pictures in case of bad weather and the coroner gets here late."

An adult white male's deceased body had been brought in by the Coast Guard from offshore and respectfully laid it on our FWC boat dock on the Barge Canal. It appeared he had passed away within hours before. The deceased man was only in his underwear, apparently having been in the water trying to fix something on a commercial fishing vessel, and sadly drowned. It was almost night, and the Lt. and I were there to secure it until the coroner and our investigator arrived. I retrieved my issued 35mm camera out of my patrol vehicle and walked back down the long stairs to the dock. We again removed the covering over the body, and I proceeded to take several pictures in case they were needed later.

The coroner arrived soon after and surprisingly was a young woman in a dress and heels. Obviously, she had been at some function and had come straight here. We three stood on the dimly lighted dock, while the coroner wearing rubber gloves and bending down proceeded to push the body with her hands in various places while closely doing her preliminary examination. I had seen a fair share of deaths of course, as well as torn up bodies from accidents. However, whether it was the look and noises the body was making with her hand pushes or the fact a woman in a dress and heels was doing this, my mind didn't like it. I began to feel woozy, and so calmly backed up and turned around. I took several deep breaths which helped a lot. I didn't want them to see my sudden dizziness.

Several months later I had to develop my film into a one-hour photo in Crystal River. In those days, we kept the roll of film and didn't develop it unless needed for court. If it wasn't needed we never developed it, we would just get another one after we filled the previous one. This was done in the district to save money. All state money had to be tracked and accounted for. (too bad the federal government wasn't that way)! I dropped the film off at the one-hour photo in Walgreens and returned an hour later. I needed some pictures off of it for a derelict vessel case only. I knew I had some undersized fish pictures on it also but only needed the derelict ones. To get those I had to develop the whole roll of course.

"Yes, sir are my pictures ready?" I asked the young adult male working behind the film counter.

He immediately grabbed a picture envelope full of pictures and negatives from a location all by itself and handed it to me with the bill. He looked a little flustered.

"I'm glad nobody else saw those pictures!"

I looked back at him puzzled. "What do you mean sir?"

"Those pictures of that dead guy! I'm glad nobody else saw them!"

I froze for a second with the realization of what he meant. I did my best to keep my composure.

"To be honest sir, that incident was several months ago. I sincerely apologize for not advising and warning you about that!"

(My sincere apologies and condolences also to that

deceased man and family of that incident, decades ago... may he be in a better place)!

~

HURRICANES ARE A TRUE WAR ZONE. I have worked many, the worst being Cat. 5 Hurricane Andrew. An aerial picture made it look like a massive biblical tornado! There is destruction and suffering by the inhabitants, and later the people called in to help. There are no alarm systems, power, or refrigeration. It was very hot and humid. This of course breeds chaos; there is a lack of food, shelter, communication, and medical aid. Initially, there are no street signs, street lights, or traffic lights, and a lot of human scumbags take advantage of it. That is why there are curfews and boat ramps are closed.

Thieves and unlicensed construction expert con artists want to take advantage of no alarms, no one home, desperate people, and a distracted police department. Many officers like me, volunteered to work these hurricanes, mainly for overtime reasons truth be told. We shoved food, clothing, toiletries, ironing boards, extra bullets, gas cans, etc... in our cars. We hitched our boats and carried extra cash in our wallets. In those days, most had no cell phones or GPS, just paper maps. We prepared for war essentially, being ready to sleep in our car, a non-powered hotel, an old military base, or even a Coast Guard Station. I have done all of that. We would convoy to the location with blue lights on, sometimes in hail, rain, and lightning, through the night. You worked 14 to 16 hr days, often night shift, and tried to sleep during the noisy days without air conditioning. Day after day and night after night, you would stand all day directing traffic. Or guard the FEMA trailers with hundreds of thousands of dollars that distributed money to some people who looked and acted like they never had a checking account in their whole lives. You had to babysit long angry lines of people, sometimes fighting each other from stress and cutting lines. There were also stacks of supplies everywhere, including huge piles of plastic water bottles. It was discovered apparently that if the water bottles stayed in the hot sun for too many days the water became unsafe for people. Later on, I noticed expiration dates stamped on them.

Many spoke different languages, and some cried tears. It was all horrible. Large military tent cities of sorts would spring up with port o potties. Convoys of Red Cross, power trucks, law enforcement, and military vehicles were to and from, while military and news helicopters flew close overhead. Near the large military tent city craziness, I bumped into fellow Officer Billy Geiger Sr. It was surreal because he was in his Special Forces military uniform on active duty for the disaster, and it all brought me back to my army days in Germany. He was a large powerful man and gave me a handshake that told me I was glad he was on our side. He was (Airborne) and served in the first Gulf War also.

Some of our Lt.s would drive around with extra tires, because of so many flats caused by destroyed roofs, the nails and screws ended up in the streets. I had two flat tires while there. They also distributed food and water to officers working traffic control in the hot sun wearing the traffic vests. I could hardly eat though while doing so, if I stopped waving my tired arm around, the people and traffic would just stop and honk their horns. It was a true hot steamy hell for all!

A quick note also of the power of hurricanes. I have seen cement buildings and entire road sections destroyed! During the Hurricane Opal detail in the Florida panhandle, I saw huge vessels of all sorts, pushed over embankments and roadways deep into people's inland property. Along the coastline, I have even seen mile-long sections of paved roadways completely flipped upside down by the pounding waves! You could see the tar side on the bottom, and layers of bedrock on top! The missing sections had to be barricaded off with flashing lights, to prevent cars from dropping off many feet down!

Anyways, I could write a book on all the conflicts, fighting, yelling, crying and accidents I witnessed during hurricane destruction over 26yrs, but I digress.

One early morning on the Hurricane Andrew detail, I went to the Miami - Dade Police station for a free quick outdoor breakfast they had started providing. Many of us stayed in Miami, where some damaged hotels eventually got power and water, and then drove back and forth in the chaos to different daily or nightly assignments in the completely destroyed and flattened Homestead area. I had to park way out, because of the hundred or so other police vehicles stretching out everywhere. In war, you eat when you can, and you sleep when you can!

I started walking and zig zagging through the sea of patrol cars with my sights on the far away food line outside. As I progressed in the already hot and humid morning, I stopped suddenly. My stomach started bubbling and making noises.

"Oh no!" I mumbled aloud to myself. I stood frozen holding my stomach. This can't be happening I thought! My roommate a fellow Officer had thrown up the night before. Due to lack of refrigeration, heat, crowds, and bad water perhaps, people were getting sick. My roommate had sweats and pukes for several hours but managed to pull through and bravely went to work the next morning. Overtime is overtime!

I stood there in horror weighing my options, I knew I had diarrhea coming soon! I had no idea where a bathroom was and was far away in the middle of a hundred police cars anyways. I had no paper in my pocket, and my stomach got worse. I quickly went to a remote spot with nobody around, and taking my gun belt off squatted low down between two cars. I even lowered my head down. I then proceeded to lay the biggest pile of liquid "Ca Ca", between two marked police cars in broad daylight, on this side of Florida! When done I waited, and another round came! I won't describe the noise or smell. I hope you are not eating! Again, I had no paper. I prayed it was over and no news helicopter was watching from a long-range camera! I eventually made it back with success to a bathroom in the area with some far walking and praying. I did a lot of cleaning and washing. Gross stuff! I don't recall where I obtained them, but those pink Pepto Bismo pills saved my life! I would have liked to be a fly on the wall when those Officers returned from breakfast and got back to their patrol cars! Haha!

~

I HEADED to our new Florida Marine Patrol station on the Barge Canal with a small trailer in tow on Hwy 19. On the trailer, were over a dozen large solid aluminum manatee idle signs, all stacked up. They were newly made and had large metal clips welded to the tops of all of them. They were a good 6' x 8' in size if I remember right. In the early '90s, gas prices were a fraction of what it is now. Although Florida was somewhat less populated then, it still had at least 17 million people, residents, with a million registered boaters. Additionally, we were told another 10 million people went back and forth as visitors. Citrus county and neighboring areas are unique in that it has a scallop season, which people love to snorkel to catch and eat. They are tasty morsels. The area where the scallops thrive is close offshore and in shallow clear water. It was a perfect family boating and swimming activity.

In the states genius (I say that sarcastically) the season opened on the 4 July weekend! To say it was chaotic was an understatement. At that time there was no speed limit in Crystal River, no summertime restrictions zones in Kings Bay, and far fewer manatee zones. Every hotel, boat ramp, dock, and nearby streets were crammed with boat trailers, vehicles, and people! People in Kings Bay and Crystal River were jet skiing, water skiing, and boating at any speed they wanted! They went back and forth from offshore, and also to the upriver clear freshwater springs. It was impossible to stop and check anyone in the waked highly turbulent river. You had to carefully proceed and hold on tight in the choppy chaos in the river and channel until you got offshore. Out there anybody familiar will tell you, was a city of hundreds and hundreds of boats! Most display the proper dive flag. They came by water as far away as Cedar Key or Weeki Wachee River! Not to mention people trailering their boats from all over the state.

If I was deep in the crowd checking licenses, flags and bag limits, etc.. it would take at least an hour to zig and zag at slow speed to get out of it. People would be snorkeling many times way past their flag area, and all had to be extremely careful! Many like us officers, smartly put their boats in the water tied to docks the morning before, so as not to deal with the crazy boat ramps.

All "days off" were canceled on holiday weekends, especially during that opening of scallop season; all hands were on deck! All did at least the required 12 hrs day or night shift. Every law enforcement agency was out there, even law enforcement aircraft. If you looked around and didn't see blue lights flashing from a vessel stop or en route to an emergency, it would have been rare!

Sometimes a call out on the VHF marine radio would hail out "Marine Patrol we need help!" After we requested their location they sometimes would say "We are offshore of Crystal River, I can see the power plant!". (That of course didn't help us much. Please get a GPS, and know how to get your LAT/LONG position! It may save your life).

Throughout the years, I developed a compressed spine from all the boat pounding. My vertebrates compressed and pinched my sciatic nerve. Sometimes I hurt so bad I had to crawl to the bathroom and prayed I didn't have to sneeze or cough! I had physical therapy many times in my life, as well as muscle relaxers and shoulder surgery. There were times I would come home, chug down half a light beer, and jump in the swimming pool with my uniform still on. In bed laying down, the bed seemed like it was moving and that I was still on water!

My point to all this, was due to all the accidents practically every hour, the county enacted a special holiday weekend only Idle Zone in Kings Bay. The bay was only seasonally slow in the wintertime back then. The job then became ours for some reason, to post the large idle signs over the winter signs already in place. Usually, myself and another officer in plain clothes the day before the holiday weekend, had to nose our boat up the sign and keep the throttle going, while the other Officer fumbled with both hands and tried to balance putting the large Idle sign in place. This was tricky with different tides and wind. Sometimes the metal edges would nick us or our boat decks, which was a bummer come time for the dreaded annual white glove equipment inspections.

I noticed over the years, that some other law enforcement agencies would mistakenly cite that violation as a "Manatee Zone" violation which was wrong. We wrote it as a "Restricted Area " violation as it was intended. A small thing of course, which in any case no doubt possibly saved lives.

While towing the new signs down Highway 19 at over 50mph, I suddenly heard a "Swoosh!". I looked in my rear view mirror, and my heart went in my throat. I saw one of the huge aluminum signs flying and spinning like a Frisbee in the air! I carefully pulled over with my blue lights on and backed up on the side of the road. Before I got close enough, a car came, and even though it slowed still ran over the newly painted sign putting fresh tire tracks on it. I truly didn't care; I was thanking God it didn't go thru someone's windshield and kill somebody! I still cringe at the thought today. No matter what I towed after that, I made damn sure it was very very secure!

~

"RINNNNGGGGGG!" I sat up quickly at the noise and groggily grabbed the phone beside me.

"Yes?"

Dispatch from Tampa on the other end replied. "Sorry to wake you, Kam. The Coast Guard from Yankeetown is offshore in your area. They are towing a large disabled Catamaran with passengers. They had been towing for hours in rough seas trying to bring it in, but now are low in fuel. They need you to meet their truck at a marina which drove up from their station. Pick up their fuel from the truck and bring it to their boat offshore. I have the Lat/Long when you are ready." (All fuel stations/marinas were closed in that remote area of Taylor County late at night).

I stumbled around and got a pen and paper. I observed it was after midnight. I had just finished my swing shift a couple of hours ago.

"Go ahead" I replied. After jotting down the numbers, I quickly went to the bathroom, drank some water, put on my now wrinkled uniform and gun belt, then headed out. I also had to grab my jacket as it was cold early winter night.

It was 1990 and I was renting a small old river house on the upper Steinhatchee River. It was very hard to find rentals on my low salary, much less on the water. My training Officer hooked me up with a landlord, a retired Federal Firearm and Tobacco Officer. Hence, I was able to keep my 23' inboard motor "Regal" patrol boat with bottom paint on his nearby dock. Luckily, I had filled up the boat at the marina before it closed at 5 PM, as was needed and required. My shift hadn't ended until 10 PM, but it still had over half a tank full.

I got into the boat and lifted the back heavy inboard motor cover off. I then hit the blower switch, which blew out any possible gas fumes. This was always required before turning the key on to avoid possibly blowing yourself up! After starting it, turning on my navigation lights, and my slow to start radar, I proceeded in the cold dark drizzling night. The boat had a hard top and windshield. It also had a manual one sided windshield wiper which I had to periodically grab with one hand and turn back and forth to see better in the dark. I then turned on my remote spotlight and swiveled it back and forth as I increased in speed. My radar hadn't warmed up all the way yet.

I never tried to be a hero with no spot light unless I was slowly sneaking around. Too many times I had seen obstacles appear in front of me at high speeds that the radar was behind on. Later on in my career, an older officer who was a true expert at navigation almost killed us by narrowly missing the power plant spoil bank. He had out ran his radar unknowingly and at the last minute turned on his spotlight, thank God. He had to whip the boat hard right at the last second to avoid the collision. The force of the turn almost threw me out! (see other officers make mistakes too).

I continued in the cold dark while sitting in my high cushioned-backed swivel chair. The boat was somewhat old but clean. Its merc-cruiser engine purred powerfully on. I met the Coast Guard truck further down the river and loaded many large heavy fuel containers. I then continued on. Out in the channel, the seas got rougher, and the rain got harder. I had to squint through the raindrops while working the spotlight, radar, windshield wiper, throttle, and LORAN. All the while keeping an eye on the compass. I was offshore of the first channel marker, but still could not the flashing lights of the Coast Guard boat yet. The Coast Guard while having a challenging and dangerous job like us, also had several people on board to help. They commonly had a boat operator, navigator, mechanic, and boarding officer. We on the other hand, usually only had one officer, which made us wary, careful, and sometimes demanding. If we give you a lawful order, please abide. We are not playing around!

"Wham!" The boat had suddenly hit a large wave, and I went flying backward! I hit the back of my head against the closed engine cover. I saw stars so to speak, and pain shot into my head. I was lying on my back with my head up against the inboard engine cover. The boat continued to slam up and down while still going forward since I stupidly had not attached the in your way kill switch. I also did not have a life jacket on. It wasn't required on the job back then, only that it was accessible in a compartment like everyone else. Rain and cold salt spray hit my face as I scrambled painfully to get up in the rocking boat, still plowing forward in the dark. I noticed also that my entire seat which had been bolted down with five bolts had ripped completely out of the deck! A large chunk of the deck was still attached to its bottom! (I learned later it had happened before with another Regal patrol boat.) Apparently, with age and our out of the ordinary water usage, it got "punky".

I managed to stagger forward and grab the throttle to slow it way down. I noticed also the Coast Guard lights flashing in the distance. About five minutes later, even though I had slowed, I semi-banged hard against the Coast Guard boat in the rough seas as I approached them. The darkness and rain had made the distance deceiving to me, but luckily they had their large rubber bumpers out. They quickly tied me off and turned the deck lights on. Their reflective orange life jackets and individual jobs were a sharp contrast to my wet, broken seat, no life jacket self. They are a true military blessing to the country. I stayed professional and helped them with the fuel containers. The huge catamaran tied behind them loomed in the dark. It looked canted in the water, perhaps having a slow leak making it even heavier. That probably was why they almost ran out of fuel. The "Coasties" as we called them, were grateful. They could now tow the stranded boat into the safety of the Steinhatchee River. They then would still have to make their way all the way back to Yankeetown, several counties away. It was going to be a long night for them! We shook hands and waved goodbye. They untied me and gave me a hard shove off in the dark and rain. I slowly plowed some distance off and stopped. I dug out my life jacket and put it on. I also hooked up my kill switch, which was hooked to myself and near the ignition key area. If I fell again, the kill switch key would pop out and shut the engine off. If I had fallen out of the boat with no life jacket and wearing my heavy gun belt while offshore, and my patrol boat continuing with no kill switch, I surely would have died! I headed home. I was wet, my head hurt badly, and I had to stand now as I now had no seat. I was thankful however to be alive, and as many times in my life, I thanked God!

~

THE JOKER HAD HEARD me on water patrol in Crystal River and called me on the talk-around channel for officers. This channel didn't go through dispatch and was meant for local officers to communicate. We didn't bother using the ten codes or signals on it much. The Joker wanted to hop on my boat for a while to get some water patrol hours and "activity". I met him at the old Knox's Bait House ramp adjacent to Hwy 19 where we commonly launched back then. I kept the boat across the street at the fire department parking lot where they let me use their outdoor water hose to wash the salt water off my boat and trailer at the end of every shift. Saltwater is incredibly corrosive which can ruin boat trailers, even zippers on jackets! I also of course had to daily check my Glock 19-9mm caliber gun for salt spray!

The Joker hopped on my assigned heavy 21' Mako marked patrol boat.

"I can only go a couple of hours, so let's stay in Kings Bay" my senior Investigator Officer advised.

I nodded my head and idled out to where the boats were hauling butt boating and water skiing back and forth around Buzzard Island in Kings Bay. We proceeded to check a few boats by doing a "BSI" (Boating Safety Inspection) form that we filled out. If the boater passed we gave out a boating safety decal they could put on their port side. It was changed annually. It wasn't required, but it let other law enforcement officers know they had already been checked that year. If we saw an excessive amount of people or they were fishing, we would still stop and check them regardless of the decal. People like to have the decal displayed prominently so to hopefully keep us away, kind of like those PBA or other donation stickers put on the back of cars to hopefully deter law enforcement stops like garlic warding off a vampire.

While patrolling we noticed a bow rider, which is seen frequently year round. A young teenager was sitting on the bow of a boat with his feet hanging over the front. There was no rail, and the adult male operator had the boat bobbing up and down a good 25mph. I gave them a short chase with blue lights and pulled them over. After throwing out our black bumpers, the Joker tied us up and began the verbal education and safety check.

"Good afternoon captain. We are with the Florida Marine Patrol. The reason why we stopped you is that bow riding is illegal. If he fell overboard (nodding towards the kid) he would most likely go under that meat grinder boat prop. There is no way you could react in time to stop it. May I see your boat registration please?"

The kid sat up and resat on the seat in front of the console. I gave the kid a smile and thumbs up. I looked around making sure we weren't drifting into anything.

"I tried to get him to sit down over here, but he wouldn't listen to me!" the boat captain declared while handing the Joker his registration.

The Joker was standing and already had his ticket book out. At the captain's statement, the Joker looked at him through his Ray-Ban sunglasses and replied fiercely.

"Well... who is bigger... you, or him?"

The man's face got beet red and sat down. The Joker sat down and completed the "Careless Operation" mail-in infraction. The Joker's statement was as usual one of a kind, but most all Marine Officers have experienced or heard of bad boat accidents involving bow-riding. For all we know, we saved that kid's life that day, as well as many others throughout time. I'd like to think so anyway.

At the end of the shift, we headed back to the boat ramp. As usual, the Joker obtained more "activity" than I did in his two hours versus my entire shift. The Italian and I working long hot holiday weekends in the past, would notice the Joker would do that same thing. We sometimes had competitions on how many BSI inspections we could get on holiday weekends. I had heard one time the Joker had radioed in exaggerated numbers of inspections, warnings, accidents, and citations at the end of his shift on a holiday weekend as required back then. Hearing the exaggerated stats on the radio, everyone else just getting started on their shift then killed themselves to at least get matching inspections! Come to find out, the Joker had lied on the radio and then quickly called the dispatcher with his real stats, a fraction of what he had said before! Damn Joker!

I pulled up to the boat ramp and hopped off. The Joker then took over, and as was common with the rare two officers on one boat, one backed the trailer down and the other would drive the boat up the trailer. The boat operator would then keep the throttle power going making the boat stay on the inclined trailer until the other Officer hooked up the trailer cable. The Joker kept the throttle going, and I hooked up the winch cable to the bow. The Joker thought I was done and quickly throttled back. I had however had not locked it down yet, causing the large heavy solid metal winch handle to slowly spin as the heavy Mako boat began to slightly slide back on the trailer. So, instead of putting my hand in the air and yelling to the Joker to keep it coming, I had the ingenious idea of reaching out towards the handle with my left hand to stop it first and then wave to the Joker with my right to keep coming.

"Crack!" With one quick turn, the heavy handle spun suddenly fast and smashed my left ring finger knuckle. My wedding crushed and the pain made me grab it and wince hard. I walked away and held it gingerly in severe pain. The Joker noticed and came to aid. After securing the boat he drove me to the Seven Rivers Hospital emergency room for treatment. There my hand had swelled up like a balloon and they had to cut my ring off. While a nurse also had to attend to some bleeding cuts I had, the Joker couldn't resist.

"Ok Kam! Bend over and cough buddy!" He said this as he grabbed a rubber glove and put it on with mock seriousness. This of course made the nearby nurses laugh as I gritted my teeth in pain. Funny now, but not then. I had to wait a week for the swelling to go down before they put a cast on. To this day I only have nine knuckles, as that one was smashed to smithereens! Luckily, I eventually was able to close my hand back and forth fully over time.

I had heard of another Officer completely losing his lower teeth from a spinning boat winch. In the past, I had seen the Italian with several spinning boat winches. He would throw both hands in the air and yell out "watch out!". I had thought at the time it was somewhat overly dramatic. I realize now he was smarter than I was!

～

To conclude my mishaps, I'd also like to briefly mention times I had in the military. A fellow Military Police Officer while we were on an emergency consecutive 12hrs/30 day night detail, accidentally discharged his 45cal pistol and shot through a small guard shack I was in! (An explosive fire extinguisher had been found on a base.) He sloppily was clearing his weapon at the end of his shift and ignored the clearing barrel as part of the process. It was close! He was expelled from Military Police to kitchen duties until his discharge.

Another time while in Army basic training, I was in the outdoor latrine at midnight. It was cold and we were training at various things for a week in the deep woods, sleeping in pup tents with little chance for sleep. I heard "Formation!" yelled out in the distance. I knew I had a minute to run there or get yelled out by drill sergeants while doing push-ups in the red clay mud and rain. So instead of going the long way around trees, I ran directly in the dark and fell face first into a pile of many rolls of razor wire! The large rolls were piled around a large unlit tree and were only marked to be visible in the daytime. I jerked up quickly and felt trickles of blood on my face, but continued to the formation. Luckily, I had winter Army clothing on, a helmet, and winter gloves, or else I would have been shredded and scarred for life, maybe even dead from blood loss.

At the formation, my uniform was in shreds and blood was on my face. Upon inspection of me by a very shocked drill sergeant, I yelled out my brief explanation. After he paused briefly he yelled "Private Johnson! Get to the supply truck for new fatigues, and back to the night convoy line! ASAP!"

Lastly, in basic training, we had to throw a live grenade at a target from behind a low thick cement wall. Our platoon all wore heavy flack jackets and helmets. We went one at a time to the wall. A safety person with a red helmet on would hand you the live grenade. You then would face the target area over the low wall. You pulled the pin and then pointed your weak hand towards the target. You also reached back with your strong hand while holding the grenade and released the spoon. Keeping that position you cooked off the grenade for several seconds, before throwing the grenade in a high arc fashion at your intended target. You then ducked down behind the wall. While others had thrown theirs before me one at a time, you could literately feel your chest bones vibrate from the explosion!

Anyways, when I pulled the pin and rocked my arm back an unexpected noise came from the grenade "Phissssssssst".

The safety suddenly yelled "Throw it now!!"

I did so and the safety threw me down and protectively jumped on top of me. I was 18 years old at the time.

After many seconds, I spoke in great concern.

"Did I do something wrong?"

"No, it ruptured! Meaning it could have gone off at any time!"

"Is that common?" I asked getting crushed by him on my stomach and struggling to breathe.

"Nawww. Happens one in a million!"

Figures I thought, leave it to me. The whole platoon including myself had to low crawl out of there. Later, I heard EOD came and exploded it manually somehow.

Back at the barracks later my MP friend whom I called "wetback" stated, "Figures it was you egghead!"

He called me that as well as" Charlie Brown' because of my shaved round head.

"Yea. Figures. But thank you God I'm still alive!"

10

SOME THINGS JUST CAN'T BE EXPLAINED

O ne day shift I got called out early to patrol offshore of the Chassahowitzka River in the Gulf of Mexico. (Locals just call it the "Chass"). A search and rescue was underway for a missing boater. We were to BOLO (be on the look out) for a small Jon boat with two white adult males that had been fishing the day before and never returned. When these things occur all hands are on the deck of course, including the Coast Guard and Sheriff's department. Frequently also, friends and family, commercial fishermen, and recreational boats listening to the broadcast given by the U.S Coast Guard on the VHF marine radio will also help and keep a lookout.

After many hours of myself and many others patrolling that area inland and offshore while looking around with powerful binoculars, that vessel still could not be found. The day was humid and calm with only a slight hot breeze. The area was also somewhat remote and at that time had very little boat traffic other than all the searchers. A lot of information is retrieved from the family with regards to the range of the missing vessel, where they launched, are the vehicle and trailer still there, do they have any communication, what was the last communication, vessel description, etc..? This information is shared by all.

Eventually, many of us paused and gathered up in a boat group in the outer channel offshore. The area of course is massive, and even taking account of the small size of the vessel there were thousands and thousands of acres of marshland that included many islands and creeks, not to mention the entire area of the Gulf of Mexico! We got in a small circle including myself, another FWC officer, Coast Guard, and a Sheriff Deputy all in separate boats. We had hoped for a flare sighting by someone, and now we were relying on the large U.S Coast Guard aircraft overhead doing a large grid search for the missing boat. A while later, the younger FWC officer new to the area spotted a large marker pole off in the distance. He decided to boat up to it and put the location in his GPS for future use at night. The water has many obstacles, including poles the locals or even Sea Tow will pound down to mark a rocky and shallow area. It is important to know your area, especially at night. By putting them in your GPS it will display at night when cruising around.

The younger Officer sped off in that direction at high speed, and not more than a few minutes later I heard on my FWC radio.

"480 Crystal River."

"Go ahead 480" the dispatcher quickly replied.

"I located the two missing fishermen by channel marker 3. The boat is missing, but both men are 10-4 and are in my boat safely. I'll be 10-51 inbound."

"10-4 480! I'll advise the others!"

The young officer while inbound with the men stopped briefly at our group. All were happy and relieved of course. The men sat in the back of his boat and were exhausted, wet, red with sunburn, and windblown. I handed them water to drink. They weakly advised in scratchy low voices, that they had been holding onto the marker and could actually hear our voices in the distance, but due to exhaustion and the breeze blowing against them, we could not hear their yells for help. Their boat had apparently been blown away while they were in the water swimming the day before. They were brought to shore and checked out by EMS before they were released.

This story is not over yet! Fast forward many years later, perhaps even as many as ten. My wife and I had invited our son's girlfriend and her family to our house for his high school graduation party. We had never met her family, and my wife used this opportunity to do so. Eventually, all were gathered up in our house and the father of our son's girlfriend began to relay a story. Stacey described how many years ago, after fishing all day off Chassahowitzka, he and his buddy went swimming. His fishing buddy slid quickly overboard even before the boat was fully stopped. He put the boat in neutral he thought, and also slid overboard as the boat still moved in momentum. When they both surfaced, it was realized the boat had not been fully in neutral! To make matters worse, a few clouds and a cooler breeze suddenly brought up a burst of wind which is common offshore in the huge open waters. Stacey swam quickly for the runaway boat, but only managed to reach out and get slight cuts from the still moving outboard motor prop. The boat was still in gear and propelling forward with a wind blowing it also. They watched it leave them as they were left in water too deep to stand!

They then had no choice but to swim about 3/4 of a mile to the closest thing in the Gulf to grab a hold of. The channel markers for Chass are old and in an erratic line. Many of the offshore ones are rarely used except by the large boats. Most of the boats used in that remote area are shallow draft boats and leave the channel earlier to get to their destinations in the shallow water.

Stacey continued, "We were in water still too deep to stand and breathe, and so we swam to Channel Marker Three. We were able to take turns during the night and rotate standing in the upper part of the marker. The next day, we managed to break a large piece of the board off and use it as a teeter-totter of sorts, for each of us to sit out of the water. When the young FWC officer headed out towards that pole that next day, he had looked off toward our direction. He told us later at that time he didn't see us, but was puzzled at how us sitting on that homemade teeter totter apparently, had made it look like a giant Cross in the distance!"

When he told that story, I of course was amazed! He did not recognize me at the time, nor did I him. He only had seen my patrol truck in the yard no doubt and relayed the incident. He concluded with, "Apparently I still have a purpose to fulfill. I guess it wasn't my time!"

I suddenly exclaimed in amazement, "That was you?!"

A few years later, Stacey's daughter and my son got married. I now have two grandkids and one more on the way from them. I recently spoke with Stacey and got permission to relay this story. He also revealed more that I thought was very interesting. Apparently, about a week after the incident, his runaway boat was spotted practically in the middle grounds off Steinhatchee in the Gulf. A boater had seen a flock of birds roosting on something way offshore. When he investigated, it was indeed the missing boat. The boater towed it into Steinhatchee, where with the help of the Coast Guard and its registration, contacted Stacey. Stacey drove up there and actually boated around Steinhatchee with it, before towing it back home many Counties away.

Steinhatchee was my first duty assignment, his daughter married my son, a sign of the "Cross" saved Stacey, and he still has the boat today. "Some things cannot be explained...!"

11

MY FTOS (FIELD TRAINING OFFICERS) AND ANGRY CUSTOMERS

A FTO *is special. He or she is one who shows a recruit the real deal. It's where the rubber meets the road. Like a parent, his/her training can imprint that recruits behavior on the job for the rest of their career. The FTO, for most of my career, didn't get paid anything extra for the job. Additionally, the FTO had to fill out a mountain of paperwork daily and weekly on the recruit. For three months the FTO, instead of doing his or her own thing freely, now has to daily explain and show the "Rookie" everything! The recruit's career is in the hands of the FTO, and a lot of liability during and after the training is on the FTO. The FTO had to have extra training, and the program was voluntary. I became one later in my career, but I got a pay increase, just for the three-month period.*

"Holly Molly!" I said to myself quietly aloud in the wind. I was sitting on the bench seat hunkering down behind the windshield. I gripped a console pole tightly with one hand and the seat with the other.

"Hang on!" my older second Field Training Officer "Glen Rogers" advised loudly. He was operating his assigned marked 21' Answer patrol boat. The 225 hp outboard motor was screaming in protest as he punched it to the max and trimmed it up even further. As I looked around, I actually saw tall water birds walking around not 20' away off to the sides of us before flying away in terror. Not for the faint of heart! No other human being I thought except Glen could be capable of chasing down an airboat in this shallow and dangerous waters off Suwannee Sound in Levy County, while in a 21' motorboat! Glen was one of the oldest officers in the district, and he knew these waters like he knew his backyard.

We had on our blue lights and even hit the very loud air horn to try to stop the airboat with three adult male passengers on board. The airboat was punching it loudly also while going inbound, but Glen had come in at an angle to cut it off, and after a minute of ridiculous side by side high speed operating, they could not fake ignore us any longer.

"Florida Marine Patrol! Shut it off now!" my training officer demanded loudly.

As they did so, I threw out our three tied together rubber black bumpers and reached over the side to grab the airboat and cleated it off to us. We were adrift and in the middle of nowhere. Nothing and nobody was around but saltwater, small islands of saw grass, and the marshy land off to the East less than two miles away. We could have easily got out and walked around in the 18inches or less of water. It was only inches deep in sporadic places nearby!

"Why didn't you stop earlier? Don't you know it's a Felony to " Flee and Allude" law enforcement?!" I asked sternly and loudly.

Like Glen, I was aggravated at the dangerous chase down. Glen, now also having the airboat in tow was busy backing us up and making sure we stayed in navigable water. Luckily the tide was coming in. He also was letting me do the talking, checking, and writing as I was nearing my last phase of training. Soon I would be going to my primary training officer one more time to do my last week. They gave me the usual excuses and then I checked their large tied down cooler at the bottom of the boat. It contained nine illegal sized redfish! Also at that time, you only were allowed one, and the season at that time was also closed to redfish. Long story short, since they had tried to run away from us and knew their guilt, I wrote each person three misdemeanor tickets. It was a lot of writing. It ended up in the weekly report, and our Lt. advised us both, "That was a good lick!"

~

GLEN and I had stopped a small runabout in the Suwannee River on a busy weekend. We were tied up to it and doing a routine safety equipment and registration check. Due to the current and other boat traffic, Glen maneuvered us to the shoreline where I lowered our anchor. After the check, I ended up writing a UBC (Uniform Boating Citation). As I was writing, the subject who was the only one in the boat got more and more visibly angry.

Have you ever seen a grown man, and not under the influence of anything, reach up and grab a tree branch, put the branch in his mouth, and start growling and biting it ferociously? Glen and I have! Just shortly before, I had conversed respectfully with him fine. There was no alcohol smell, no indication of mental issues, no eye pupil constrictions or dilation, etc. I had explained it was only one mail in infraction, it wasn't going to affect his driving record, and I was going to give the other several violations a verbal warning only. However, as I was writing, he grabbed the branch and angrily bit and shook it like a dog while growling! Yes, growling! I looked up in surprise at him and then at Glen who was staring in shock with his mouth open. After a half minute of this, Glen looked at me and shrugged. I then lowered my head and kept writing.

~

ONE LAST INTERESTING day with my second FTO Glen. We again were doing a routine safety check on a nice young couple on the Suwannee River. They had passed, and so I was giving them a safety decal. Upon completion, as I had told them, I now needed to check their two spotted seatrout in a bucket for legal length. As I measured the fish, I noticed the contents had a strong bleach smell.

"Do guys know this water in the fish bucket seems to have bleach in it?" I asked curiously.

"Oh yes, we do!"

I continued as you can imagine. "Were you planning on eating these fish?"

"Yes, of course! We are from out of the area, and other campers said the water here is contaminated, and so we put a little bleach in the ice water to kill all the germs."

(No dear reader....I'm not kidding).

"Ahhhhhh. I wouldn't eat those fish now folks. I haven't heard of anything in these waters that would hurt you, especially if cooked properly. I know, however, while I was in the Army, a soldier almost successfully committed suicide by ingesting bleach!"

"So we shouldn't eat these fish now?"

"Nope. Go home and bury them." (I may have saved two lives that day)!

~

"WHY CAN'T you guys leave me alone! Go get a donut or go after real criminals!"

My self and my primary FTO Officer Kevin McCroan was in his assigned 24' T-Craft with twin engines offshore of Taylor County in the Gulf of Mexico. I was in my last FTO week where I did everything while my FTO officer became a fly on a wall and evaluated. Just my luck, the first stop encompassed many safety violations and a very angry boat captain. I had stated I was going to give him several written warnings, and only cite one mail-in infraction to him. He still didn't like it! I put my head slightly down and kept writing. I of course looked occasionally up to make sure he wasn't going to get violent.

"Cripes! Can't a guy enjoy a &*^$# day of fishing anymore!" Out of the corner of my eye, I could see my training officer sitting to the side with a look of boredom and an uninterested attitude. He would casually look off into the distance. My customer cranked up the heat. He began to get more brazen and courageous. He must have sensed my nervousness, or noticed my brand new rookie uniform.

"Is this F@#$%^& America or what!" He had raised his voice more and leaned forward while glaring hard at me.

Truth be told I was nervous, perhaps even having a slight hand tremor. I had been stressing all week antici-pating this week. I had been trained well. I also had been a Military Policeman in the Army for three years as mentioned before, where I made arrests routinely for DUI, Larceny, Accidents, Domestics, etc..at an even younger age. I was now 24 years of age during my FTO training. The difference now was that my younger brother and I had quit our jobs in Melbourne and risked all moving to this area of my assignment after the academy. We roomed together and shared expenses, living paycheck to paycheck. He did odd jobs at long distances while attending the Withlacoochee Technical school. My divorced family up north had their own problems and couldn't help us. We were all on our own. We had no safety net. It was now all or nothing! All these things flashed across my mind, as I stressed about violating

policy, laws, procedures, and my FTO's opinion on passing
or failing. I wanted and needed this job badly! It was my
dream!

A calm voice of steel was suddenly heard, "Kam!
When you get done with that citation, go ahead a flip your
ticket over, and make those other warnings a ticket also!"

My angry customer and I paused a second at the
surprise of the sudden full attention of my glaring FTO.

"What!!! You can't f@#$%^& do that!" my customer
retorted.

My FTO fired back, "My partner was giving you warnings, but your attitude indicates you aren't taking him
seriously! So apparently you need more of our attention
to get compliance!"

My customer grumbled meekly and sat back while
looking embarrassed and staring off into the distance. I
completed more citations and still gave him a verbal
warning on a couple of other violations. I was tired of
writing and wanted to break away. I had him sign the
copies and explained his options and requirements for the
infractions. I started to take control of the boat, but my
FTO grabbed the controls and idled away carefully as we
do before punching it. I became nervous again because I
was now supposed to do everything, and I thought
suddenly that perhaps Kevin was disappointed with my
performance.

Before punching the boat forward at high speed,
Kevin turned and smiled at me. He waved one arm
around in the air saying "Don't sweat this last FTO week
thing, Kam. We will breeze thru it, and you will be fine!"

He then punched the large twin engine patrol boat forward like it was a part of him. (I had been with him when he towed a huge injured Minke Whale with it and Sea World to shore with that boat). We looked for offshore targets to check, and faced the challenges of the day, not as FTO and recruit, but now as brother Officers.

AFTERWORD
CONCLUSION

If you are young, healthy, have a clean record and like the outdoors, and also have a lot of initiative, then the FWC is for you. If you believe in protecting God's creations, people, fish, wildlife, and the environment; if you want the chance to make a difference, and to experience everything from whales, fish, danger, day and night shifts, storms, wildlife, people from all over the world, then this job is for you. However, if you want to get rich, cannot tell the truth all the time even if it makes you look foolish, have no empathy for people, cannot work by yourself when always outnumbered, or you are not brave, then your path in life may lie elsewhere.....

~

" *Hey you! Rookie. You should have let us sleep. Cause when you leave this lovely place, your FTO will be in your face! My car is dirty. My boat needs waxin. Don't you think about relaxin! You start to leave, I hear you squeakin. Come back Rookie, your bearings need greasin. There's water to patrol, there's coffee to drink. Shut up Rookie, who told you to think? As you start on your way tomorrow, Rookie, is another day!"*

(FTO's) unknown author. Given at Academy.

COMMON Q & A

"Thank you dear reader for taking a chance on this book! These are common questions I was asked while on duty years ago and my answers. While I believe this will be insightful and helpful to Florida fishermen and boaters, please know that regulations change and it's your responsibility to pick up the current one or contact the local FWC office, or go on line at myfwc.com. Let's be careful out there! In God We Trust!"

Q: What kind of license do I need to fish in brackish water?

A: Brackish water is a fresh/saltwater combo where a freshwater river combines with the salty sea. Both fresh and saltwater fish can be found in it. If you intend to keep and put freshwater fish only in your bucket, then you need a freshwater license. The same with saltwater fish. If you want to keep both, then you need the combo license. Out in the Gulf, only the saltwater license is acceptable.

Q: Does my wife need a fishing license if she is reading next to me fishing?

A: No. However, you do need a license to cover all the bag limits. If I check you guys coming in and you kept two bag limits, then you need a license to cover each bag limit. We can only go by what we see. You then will be charged for over the bag limit because you only have one license on board.

Q: What is the difference between IDLE speed and Slow speed zones?

A: Idle speed is when you just barely put your boat in forwarding gear only. Slow speed is faster, but your boat has to be completely "settled" in the water with your bow being level and not throwing a wake. You need to be able to make headway of course, and so you can increase your speed slightly if you are fighting the wind and tide going against you. (Since this is a tell-all book, I also have to say there have been times in horrendous torrents of rain and lightning popping all around us, that I've seen waves of boats during scallop season ignore all and punch it all the way up river to safety. I was right behind them blowing all the zones also! I believe in human life over manatees in that situation).

Q: When do I have to report a boating accident?

A: The requirement occurs generally when the total property damage exceeds $2000.00 total, missing persons, or injury beyond first aid. You can contact any legit Florida law enforcement, Sherriff's Office, etc. Again, when in doubt cover your butt and report it! Also, get the Complaint/Offense Incident number from the Officer. You will need this if you want a copy of the report later for insurance or court reasons.

Q: What is the difference between" Fork length" and" Total length" when measuring a fish

A: To properly measure a fish, lay it flat "on top" of the measuring tape. Then measure the fish from the nose to its squeezed tail. That is total length. Fork length is similar, except with fish that have a forked tail like a Mackerel or a Cobia you would measure from the nose to the fork. The Fork is the bottom of the V shape.

Q: Why do Mullet frequently jump out of the water?

A: It's because they don't want to "Fart" in their home area... LOL (old Marine Patrol Joke.)

Q: Is there an allowance for possible ice shrinkage of fish?

A: No Officer I know would allow for that remote possibility. However, supervisors, the court, and especially the Officer have no desire to write " Chicken Shit Tickets". A one-time minor offense usually warrants a warning, unless you have been warned before. If you are not sure when measuring, take a quick picture and throw it back. It's better for everyone!

Q: Does the safety and lighting requirements change in State vs Federal waters?

A: Florida has adopted the same regulations as the U.S Coast guard with regards to safety equipment, rules of the road, and navigation light requirements. This is true for both sides of Florida. This is why we carry a Coast Guard Rule book also. When we write somebody for insufficient life jackets, or "Failure to Keep a Proper Lookout" in an accident, for example, we write Florida's enabling statute that has adapted the U.S Coast Guard regulations (used to be F.S. 327.50) then we write the Coast Guard's CFR or rule number for that particular violation.

Q: I'm confused about the channel markers.

A: In general, remember "Red Right Return". This means keeping the red markers on your right when you come in from offshore. You do have to be careful, being on the wrong side may cause you to hit rocks. Also, some smaller rivers have only homemade type markers. When in doubt, go slow and watch other boaters. A navigation chart of an area gives a lot of information!

Lastly, if you are using a non digital compass to guide you, make sure you don't have something next to it that causes the needle to go way off. I realized this one day when I put my handheld radio on my boat console and watched my compass turn immediately halfway around!"

(Note: A cell phone will also affect it)!

JUST FOR FUN; NO HUMAN TRAGEDY SHOWN HERE!

Newspaper articles are from the "Citrus County Chronicle."

While coming in with my 21' Mako, I felt a bump.
An unmarked FMP officer behind me saw what I hit and
grabbed it out of the water.

My prop obviously freshly killed it. (Yes, I ate it!)

Kings Bay 1993

I pulled up to a boat that had this little hairy guy on the Crystal River. The occupants quickly stated they had a permit for it, which I was ignorant to at the time. When I asked to take his picture, they quickly handed him to me and said, we'll take a picture of you! I showed a copy of it to Captain Tucker at the office. He posted it on the bulletin board with a notice saying: which one is the monkey?

"Which one is the monkey?"

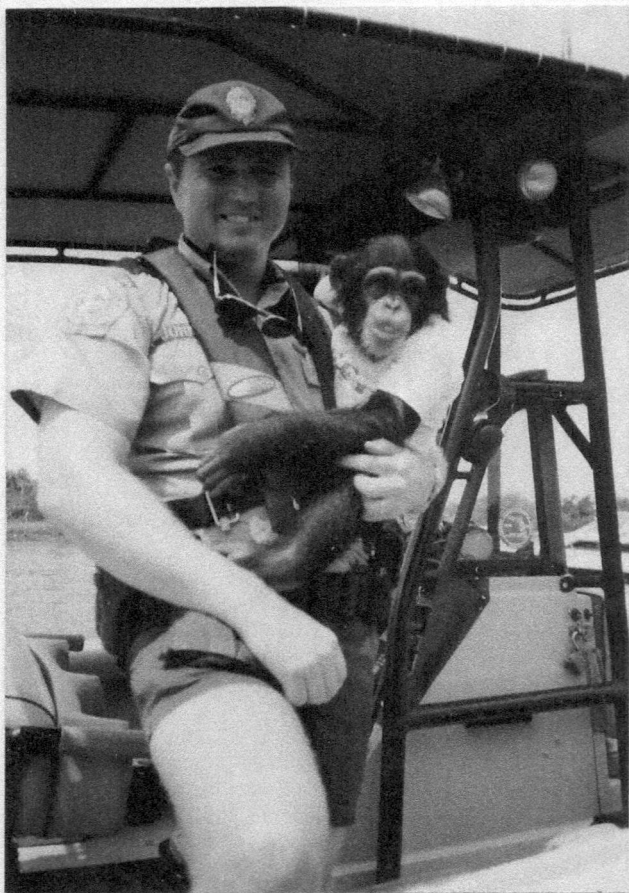

One of many, many fish cases I made at the "Redfish Hole."

"Redfish Hole"

Famous long time dispatcher and office expert Keith
Miritello. Picture is from 1983!
(I was in my first year of the Army then.)

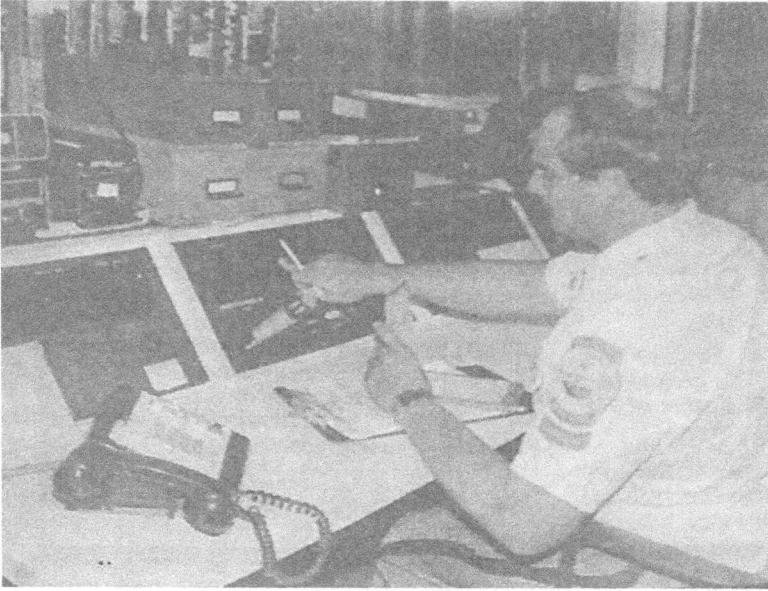

Keith Miritello 1983

A fire occurred near our FWC office one day by the Barge Canal. I called it in. Officer Thomason arrived, as well as this one lady driving the fire truck from Inglis area. Captain Tucker arrived soon after and took the picture. Funny!

Barge Canal

My Primary FTO Officer

Kevin McCroan 1990

Officer Frank Demartino and I at the yearly Homosassa River raft race.

Homosassa River

Ariel View - Homosassa River Raft Race

When not out patrolling local waters, Florida Marine Patrol officer Ham Johnson works out of the new facility just south of Inglis along the Cross Florida Barge Canal.

Florida Marine Patrol christens new home

By Greg Erbstoesser
Staff writer

After years of living out of rented quarters, the local office of the Florida Marine Patrol finally has its own home.

Construction began last May on the $850,000 complex that is, in part, tied into the eventual development of a state

stoned to follow the canal route all the way across the state to the East Coast.

The new marine patrol office complex has a new, state-of-the-art radio communications center, complete with a backup generator.

My missing knuckle hand (From a spinning boat winch), and holding a very old telescope from my great, great, great, great grandfather Captain Valentine Bagley's sea chest.

He is related thru my dad's mothers' side who was a Hathaway. The lineage can easily be proven, but I will try to be brief and close this book with the poem that immortalized him.

The captain's sea chest and contents have been distributed among my family. My sister has a lot of the very old letters that were in the chest, and my father Reginald Johnson still has the chest.

The captain born in Massachusetts in 1773, became shipwrecked in Arabia, July 10, 1792. After great suffering, there are many stories and journals that described him returning to Essex, Massachusetts where he was born and then buried at 66 years of age.

He dug a famous well. "The Captains Well." He vowed no man would suffer from thirst as he had.

Pictures are online.

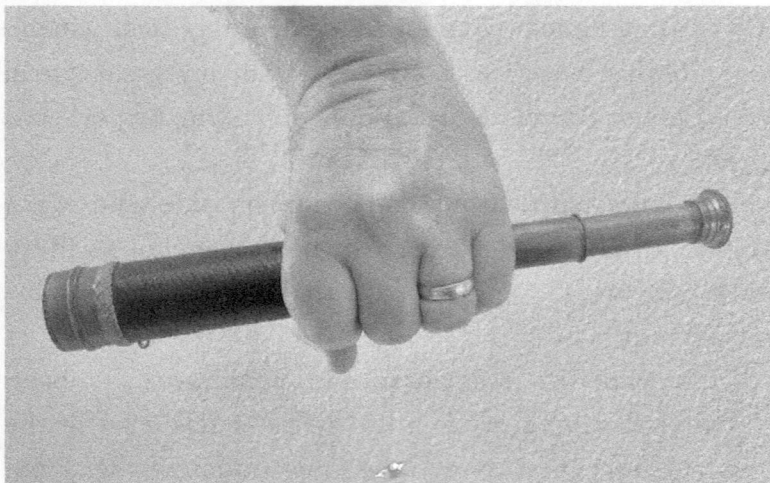

A POEM
"THE CAPTAIN'S WELL"

Written by John Greenleaf Whittier in 1889, based on
"A Journal of Travels and Sufferings of Daniel Saunders
Jr."
A castaway with also young Valentine Bagley and others,
off the Coast of Arabia, July 10, 1772.
(The journal is available online.)

From pain and peril, by land and main,
The shipwrecked sailor came back again;
And like one from the dead, the threshold cross'd
Of his wondering home, that had mourned him lost.
Where he sat once more with his kith and kin,
And welcomed his neighbors thronging in.
But when morning came he called for his spade.
"I must pay my debt to the Lord," he said.
"Why dig you here?" asked the passer-by;
"Is there gold or silver the road so nigh?"

"No, friend," he answered: "but under this sod
Is the blessed water, the wine of God."
"Water! the Powow is at your back,
And right before you the Merrimac,
"And look you up, or look you down,
There 's a well-sweep at every door in town."
"True," he said, "we have wells of our own;
But this I dig for the Lord alone."
Said the other: "This soil is dry, you know.
I doubt if a spring can be found below;
"You had better consult, before you dig,
Some water-witch, with a hazel twig."
"No, wet or dry, I will dig it here,
Shallow or deep, if it takes a year.
"In the Arab desert, where shade is none,
The waterless land of sand and sun,
"Under the pitiless, brazen sky
My burning throat as the sand was dry;
"My crazed brain listened in fever dreams
For plash of buckets and ripple of streams;
"And opening my eyes to the blinding glare,
And my lips to the breath of the blistering air,
"Tortured alike by the heavens and earth,
I cursed, like Job, the day of my birth.
"Then something tender, and sad, and mild
As a mother's voice to her wandering child,
"Rebuked my frenzy; and bowing my head,
I prayed as I never before had prayed:
"Pity me, God! for I die of thirst;
Take me out of this land accurst;

"And if ever I reach my home again,
Where earth has springs, and the sky has rain,
"I will dig a well for the passers-by,
And none shall suffer from thirst as I.
"I saw, as I prayed, my home once more,
The house, the barn, the elms by the door,
"The grass-lined road, that riverward wound,
The tall slate stones of the burying-ground,
"The belfry and steeple on meeting-house hill,
The brook with its dam, and gray grist mill,
"And I knew in that vision beyond the sea,
The very place where my well must be.
"God heard my prayer in that evil day;
He led my feet in their homeward way,
"From false mirage and dried-up well,
And the hot sand storms of a land of hell,
"Till I saw at last through the coast-hill's gap,
A city held in its stony lap,
"The mosques and the domes of scorched Muscat,
And my heart leaped up with joy thereat;
"For there was a ship at anchor lying,
A Christian flag at its mast-head flying,
"And sweetest of sounds to my homesick ear
Was my native tongue in the sailor's cheer.
"Now the Lord be thanked, I am back again,
Where earth has springs, and the skies have rain,
"And the well I promised by Oman's Sea,
I am digging for him in Amesbury."
His kindred wept, and his neighbors said
"The poor old captain is out of his head."

But from morn to noon, and from noon to night,
He toiled at his task with main and might;
And when at last, from the loosened earth,
Under his spade the stream gushed forth,
And fast as he climbed to his deep well's brim,
The water he dug for followed him,
He shouted for joy: "I have kept my word,
And here is the well I promised the Lord!"
The long years came and the long years went,
And he sat by his roadside well content;
He watched the travellers, heat-oppressed,
Pause by the way to drink and rest,
And the sweltering horses dip, as they drank,
Their nostrils deep in the cool, sweet tank,
And grateful at heart, his memory went
Back to that waterless Orient,
And the blessed answer of prayer, which came
To the earth of iron and sky of flame.
And when a wayfarer weary and hot,
Kept to the mid road, pausing not
For the well's refreshing, he shook his head;
"He don't know the value of water," he said;
"Had he prayed for a drop, as I have done,
In the desert circle of sand and sun,
"He would drink and rest, and go home to tell
That God's best gift is the wayside well!"

ABOUT THE AUTHOR

In 1983 I graduated High School, and as I had no car or college money, I enlisted in the U.S Army for three years as a Military Policeman. I was stationed in Germany and then Alabama.

During which, among other things, I received a rare German silver marksmanship award, with special orders to be able to wear it on my dress uniform.

In basic training, I was the only one in the company who tested 40 out of 40 with the M16 rifle.

On the way to walk up to receive the plaque reward, an African American drill sergeant stepped out of formation to give me a high five. As I was 18-yrs old and fresh off a remote small town farm, he had to show me what that was. I was embarrassed at my ignorance.

After an honourable discharge I drove to Florida; everything I owned was in my car. I had a total of $800.00 in cash.

I used my Army collage fund to obtain an AA degree, and then completed some criminal justice classes at UCF. During this time I worked various part time jobs. In 1989, I entered and graduated from the State of Florida Marine

Patrol Academy, as a State Law Enforcement Officer. I also became a born again Christian soon after.

We all sin everyday, but I know where I'm going after death.

Later, it changed to Florida Fish and Wildlife Commission. I became a Field Training Officer, and obtained several plaques and awards in my career. One of which was the "Officer of the Year" award in the year 2000.

After 26 years as a State Officer, I retired after having shoulder surgery. I married my better half 30 years ago. My wife, (a RN) is the smartest woman I know. We have two awesome children.

Our son is a HVAC Tech, involved in church with his wife and kids. Our daughter is a Surgical RN and is engaged to my future son-in-law.

The Lord has surely blessed me in so many ways!

ALSO BY KAM R. JOHNSON

INDEFINITE DETENTION - (Fiction, based on the 80's.Funny/dramatic/action/inspirational) eBook and Paperback on Amazon.

WINTER BLIND - (Fiction Short 5K story, dramatic/action/inspirational. Not for children. Dedicated to fellow L.E Officers) Ebook only on Amazon.

Upcoming release(s):

THE PATRIOTIC CHICKEN - (Children's story. Short fiction, Christian, patriotic, funny, inspirational.) Hardcover only, *coming winter 2022.*

www.ingramcontent.com/pod-product-compliance
Lightning Source LLC
Chambersburg PA
CBHW021425180326
41458CB00001B/132